WORLD WAR II POSTERS

DAVID POLLACK

Schiffer Publishing Ltd®
4880 Lower Valley Road • Atglen, PA 19310

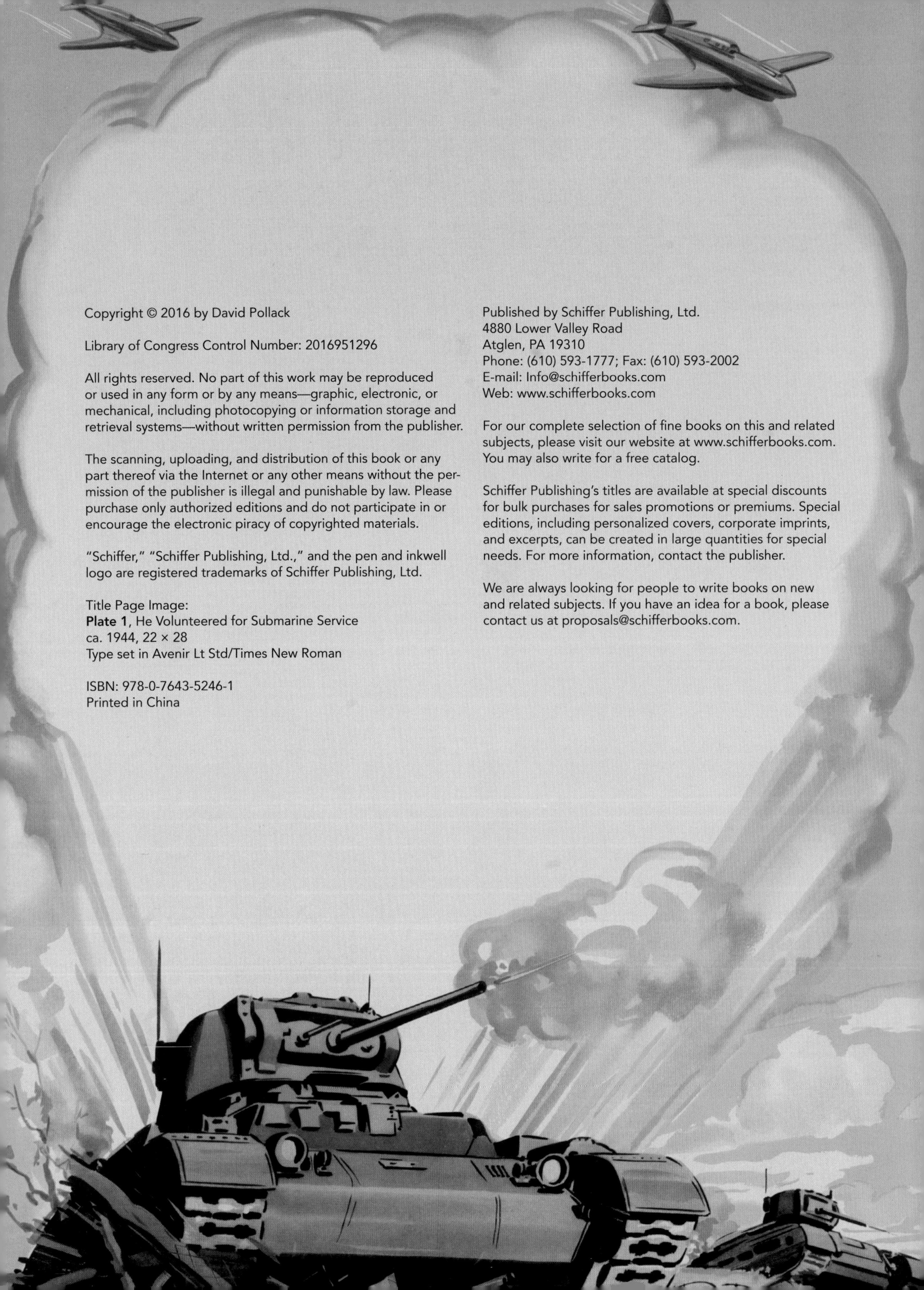

Title Page Image:
Plate 1, He Volunteered for Submarine Service
ca. 1944, 22 × 28
Type set in Avenir Lt Std/Times New Roman

ISBN: 978-0-7643-5246-1
Printed in China

Published by Schiffer Publishing, Ltd.
4880 Lower Valley Road
Atglen, PA 19310
Phone: (610) 593-1777; Fax: (610) 593-2002
E-mail: Info@schifferbooks.com
Web: www.schifferbooks.com

For our complete selection of fine books on this and related subjects, please visit our website at www.schifferbooks.com. You may also write for a free catalog.

Schiffer Publishing's titles are available at special discounts for bulk purchases for sales promotions or premiums. Special editions, including personalized covers, corporate imprints, and excerpts, can be created in large quantities for special needs. For more information, contact the publisher.

We are always looking for people to write books on new and related subjects. If you have an idea for a book, please contact us at proposals@schifferbooks.com.

For Katie, James, and Lucy
Keep learning, enjoying, and most importantly, preserving history.

CONTENTS

ACKNOWLEDGMENTS

Among the great joys of being a poster dealer is the almost daily opportunity to learn something new about history and the pleasure of actually touching and owning (if only for brief periods) items that are integral to the course of mankind. War posters, while documents of the worst events in man's history, are also relics of the best ways people behave. They offer ugliness and beauty, good and evil, destruction and salvation. The preservation of these documents is an important part in keeping the narrative of an era from being lost.

Having spent the past twenty-five years learning many facets of the world of posters—graphics, production, printing processes, preservation, etc.—has required the guidance and support of so many other dealers and professionals in the worlds of art and antiques. Among those who have shared their many years of experience and knowledge are Robert Chisholm, Chisholm-Larsson Gallery; and Gail Chisholm, Chisholm Gallery. Robert, to whom I sold the very first poster I ever found, has offered me endless information from his vast mental inventory of posters and his knowledge of just about everything. Gail, my partner in Poster Fairs International, has given of her time, inventory, and professional guidance, and on more than one occasion provided a place to stay in New York City.

Without the patience of my wife and children Lucy, Katie, and James, I would never have been able to make every vacation and journey include small side trips to antique shows, shops, flea markets, dealers' and clients' homes, and galleries. Without Lucy this book would never have been completed. In addition to doing endless research, her help was critical in so much of the book, from the selection of posters to the layout, historical concepts, and more.

Without the endless support of my clients—private collectors, fellow dealers, institutions, libraries—I would never have survived long enough as a dealer to build a business that continues to grow. This truly is a labor of love; the esoteric emails at 2 a.m. between a client or dealer and me is never a problem. It is great to hear from someone with more knowledge than I about an obscure WWII women's organization or about who published a series of VD posters in 1943, or about the subtle translation of a French poster that is an inside joke only understood by a native speaker.

So thank you all—Lucy, Katie, James, Robert, Gail, and everyone else who has helped give me the opportunity to spend enough time with posters to make this book possible.

David Pollack

INTRODUCTION

The posters of WWII are often dismissed as lackluster stepsisters of WWI posters. This is an unfortunate and unfair assumption, as the posters of WWII include numerous powerful graphics and moving illustrations created by prominent artists and anonymous designers alike.

> From a practical point, they (war posters) were used to encourage all Americans to help with the war effort. The posters called upon every man, woman, and child to endure the personal sacrifice and domestic adjustments to further the national agenda. They encouraged rationing, conservation, and sacrifice. In addition, the posters were used for recruitment, productivity, and motivation, as well as for financing the war effort. The stark, colorful graphic designs elicited strong emotions. The posters played to the fears, frustrations, and faith in freedoms that lingered in people's minds during the war.[1]

This wonderful description applies not just to American posters, but also to those of Allied and Axis countries. The fundamental need to market war was never more significant than in the global conflict of WWII.

In 1942, *Artists for Victory*, in collaboration with the Council for Democracy and the Museum of Modern Art in New York, held a national war poster competition. The competition included eight categories: Production, War Bonds, The Nature of the Enemy, Loose Talk, Slave World – Or Free World, The People are on the March, Deliver Us From Evil, and Sacrifice. These eight themes perfectly describe the issues traditionally facing a world at war and the horrors and atrocities specific to WWII.

> This competition received 2,224 entries, of which 200 were exhibited first at MOMA and then circulated nationwide, including a major exhibition at the National Gallery of Art in Washington, DC. On November 16, 1942, in a congratulatory letter to *Artists for Victory*, Franklin D Roosevelt described the competition as "proof of what can be done by groups whose ordinary occupations might seem far removed from the war. More than two thousand war posters were produced by the artists of the country, not as a chore that they were asked to do but as a voluntary, spontaneous contribution to the war. The very name of your organization is symbolic of the determination of every man and woman in every activity of life throughout the nation to enlist in the cause to which our country is dedicated."[2]

As can be seen from the volume of entries to the MOMA competition, the total number of WWII posters created was enormous. Posters were printed by the Allied countries, including the United States, Great Britain, Canada, Australia, New Zealand, and others. Posters were also printed by the Axis nations, primarily Germany, Japan, and Italy. In addition to posters printed by government agencies, thousands of posters were privately printed by societies, relief organizations, and corporations interested in providing support to the war effort. These posters may have been printed in extremely small quantities for limited distribution to a select number of facilities or printed in the tens and hundreds of thousands for the wide-scale recruiting needs of the war. This book is far from a comprehensive catalog of every poster printed; what is shown is a broad range of material, an overview of the subjects, styles, and graphics used by a variety of creators in an effort to give a wide representation and better understanding of the sensibilities of the era as expressed through posters.

Although this book is categorized by nation of origin, hopefully the reader will see similarities in subject matter and iconography used. These similarities are not limited to one side or the other, as great propaganda can be successful no matter one's personal views. In the case of war posters, the goal is to instill patriotism and support for the war effort. Through the lens of time, it is easy to say that "we" portrayed "ourselves" as heroic and honorable, with the enemy accurately portrayed as evil, while "they" used false and ugly propaganda. The reality is the tools and design sensibilities used by the artists and designers on both sides were very similar.

In addition to the obvious categories of posters from WWII, this book also includes sections devoted to specialized areas of interest. "Women and the War," the "Minority Experience," and privately printed posters will group together posters with examples that might otherwise be included in more traditional categories, such as recruiting, conservation, and production, but which come together to show a broader picture of one sector of society.

The Axis powers did create numerous posters; this book includes a very limited number of examples. These are shown to give the reader a frame of reference to the global use of propaganda and its thematic similarities.

The exact beginning and end dates for what can be defined as a WWII poster are difficult to quantify. One can use the specific dates September 1, 1939, and the German invasion of Poland with British and French declaring war on September 3 as the official beginning of the war. Likewise, May 8, 1945 (V-E Day), and August 15, 1945 (V-J Day), are recognized as the end of the war. Political and military actions before and following actual hostilities caused the creation of numerous posters outside these dates that are inexorably tied to the war and thus truly are WWII posters.

The earliest posters shown in this book are campaign posters supporting Adolph Hitler's Nazi Party and Benito Mussolini's Fascist Party. If recruiting, production, morale, and other posters created during the actual period of combat contributed to a successful end of the war, it can be argued that these two extraordinary examples of powerful graphic design were significant factors in the onset of the war (see Plates 486 and 487).

During the pre-war period of the early 1930s, Japanese aggression and expansionist desires were clear. Its 1931 invasion of Manchuria and 1933 secession from the League of Nations were the first steps towards what would later become the Pacific theater of WWII.

By the mid-1930s, the winds of war were clearly blowing globally, with various government and private organizations promoting increases in military spending and preparation. Recruiting and other posters from this period are included as part of the full context of the war. By 1934, Winston Churchill's editorials addressed his concerns about Germany's military strength:

> I marvel at the complacency of ministers in the face of the frightful experiences through which we have all so newly passed. I look with wonder upon the thoughtless crowds disporting themselves in the summer sunshine, and upon this unheeding House of Commons, which seems to have no higher function than to cheer a Minister; [and all the while across the North Sea], a terrible process is astir. Germany is arming.[3]

Posters created following the official cessation of combat are included when clearly part of the war effort or resulting from specific events in the war. Numerous posters were issued for occupying US troops stationed in Japan, the South Pacific, and Europe. Of particular interest are the diverse personal health posters issued warning of the risks and results of catching venereal diseases (see Plate 103). Posters dated after the Japanese surrender aboard the USS *Missouri* on September 2, 1945, can nonetheless be WWII posters in every sense.

Included in this book are several United States Air Force posters. The Security Act of 1947, which included the creation of the USAF as a separate branch of the United States military, was a direct outcome of the war. Prior to the creation of the Air Force, all military aviation responsibilities had been divided between the Army and Navy. During WWII, land-based operations were under the responsibility of the Army Air Corps, which was re-structured as the Army Air Forces in 1941, six months before the attack on Pearl Harbor. The Navy provided sea-based aviation from aircraft carriers and amphibious vessels.

The final section and the latest posters included in this book are a series created for the Marshall Plan (European Recovery Program). This program to rebuild Europe after the devastation of the war is possibly one of the most important efforts to result from WWII. Secretary of State George Marshall's beliefs that without such aid there would be "no political stability and no assured peace" were first expressed in his speech while receiving an honorary degree from Harvard University in June 1947.[4] The fighting had long ended and Europe was setting out on the road to recovery, but without the Marshall Plan, the consequences of the war would have lingered on for an unknown but certainly longer period of time.

The artistic qualities of posters are not all equal, and this book strives to give a broad overview of subject matter. In many cases the significance of a poster is not in its artistic merit, but rather in the content or the message. The very simple text-based 1943 poster taken from FDR's announcement of the formation of the Japanese-American 442nd Regimental Combat Team includes one of the earliest and clearest civil rights statements, "Americanism is not, and never was, a matter of race or ancestry." (It is interesting to note this poster was printed just nine months after the Japanese internment in California began. The resulting response for volunteers of Japanese ancestry was significantly higher from those living in Hawaii, where there was no internment, than it was from Japanese Americans living in the areas where internment was mandatory.) At the other end of the spectrum, Jean Carlu's "America's Answer! Production" could not be sparser of words. Although graphic design and artwork are very strong factors in the monetary value of a poster, historically significant posters showing lesser artistic sensibilities may also be important to a collection's completeness.

Supplementary information of interest and comparisons of comparable imagery are included in the poster identification section of the book.

Finally, this book is not intended as a "price guide"; it does not offer any information on values or pricing. The prices of posters are based on a number of criteria: artistic merit, subject matter, rarity, condition, artist, and more. The goal of a collector is to put together a collection of the posters that best fit their interests and pocketbook. A great collection can be built with limited resources or by spending a vast amount, but the resulting enjoyment should not be based on the money spent.

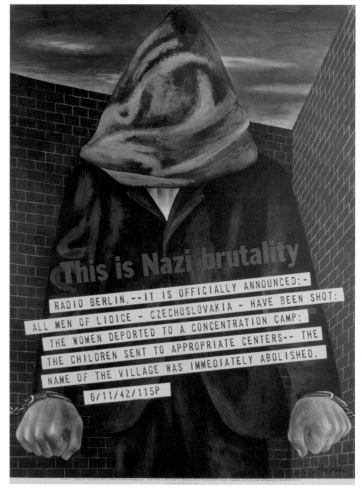

FROM PATRIOTISM TO MILITARISM
Changing Visual Imagery from WWI to WWII

In the vast realm of history, twenty-five years is barely a blip on the screen of time, but the quarter century between the First and Second World Wars saw rapid global changes in society, economics, and politics rarely seen on the time line of mankind. The Great Depression caused possibly more devastation than any event other than war in the history of man. Worldwide unemployment, poverty, and deprivation of the Depression left residual animosity and social divisions. These negative forces allowed the growth of the Third Reich, along with the empire building aspirations of Japan and fascist Italy, all of which coalesced into the atrocities of Hitler, Tojo, and Mussolini.

Propaganda posters from WWII range from cartoons urging home front gardening in support of the war cause to brutal imagery of evil and menacing caricatures of the "enemy." Graphic and violent images appear more commonly in posters of WWII than they do in posters from WWI. Whether this change in style was caused by the atrocities of the war is open for discussion, but there are sufficient examples of this to look into the motives and direction given to the artists. "Although brutality is always part of war, the atrocities of World War II were so terrible, and of such magnitude, as to engender a new category of crime—crimes against humanity."[5] These brutalities and atrocities forever changed the graphic iconography of propaganda posters.

James Montgomery Flagg described his WWI poster *I Want You!* as "the most famous poster in the world"[6]; an avuncular American symbol calmly, sternly, and forcefully urging patriotic service in the war effort. By 1940—in his *Speed Up America* created for The Committee to Defend America by Aiding the Allies—Flagg's Uncle Sam had evolved into a wild-eyed, wild-haired apparition being chased, quite literally, by a flaming swaztika.

Actual events were utilized in posters from each world war for their propaganda value. While a horrific image of a drowning mother and child is used in Fred Spear's WWI *Enlist*, it is an artistic, painterly, almost tranquil portrayal of the aftermath of the sinking of the *Lusitania*. Ben Shahn's 1942 *This is Nazi Brutality* showing the German "use of terror as a weapon"[7] was created for the US Office of War Information in direct response to the destruction of Lidice, Czechoslovakia—the massacre of all male residents of Lidice and internment of all women and children in response to the shooting of a Nazi official. The poster used the actual transcript of Radio Berlin's notification of the event "It is officially announced – All men of Lidice- Czechoslovakia – have been shot: The women deported to a concentration camp: the children sent to appropriate centers – The name of the village was immediately abolished. 6/11/42/115P." Unlike the mother and child calmly and peacefully sinking into the depths in *Enlist*, Shahn's image is of an unseen hooded, chained, and presumably terrified victim in front of a brick wall awaiting execution. Shahn's message, while strikingly similar to Spear's, is vastly different in its presentation.

Wildlife illustrator Charles Livingston Bull created powerful WWI posters featuring fish and birds. *Save the Products of the Land, Eat More Fish-They Feed Themselves* is a charming home front motivational poster with no hint of the raging war, other than the need to conserve, but the patriotic message is evident. Bull's *Be an American Eagle*, like August Hutaf's *Treat 'Em Rough*, is both clearly militaristic, yet they are both naïve in their visual portrayal of the horrors of war using metaphorical animal images as substitutions for actual humans. By WWII, rather than anthropomorphic combatants, real human beings were shown—wounded, dying, and dead.

The "so-called Great War, along with the Depression it spawned, was the driver that eventually produced the even greater catastrophe of World War II."[8] The rise of the Nazi Party and Japanese imperialism brought to the world evils not seen before, but propaganda is a tool used by all sides. It is easy to identify horrific imagery by the Allies as showing the true story and bringing out a powerful message. Similar Axis posters are viewed as nothing more than an extension of their evil deeds. This is a one-sided perception; while there is no defense of the actions of the Axis powers nor of their propaganda, it is important to recognize the similarities in iconography and imagery between Allied and Axis posters.

Artwork created by Thomas Hart Benton showing a stylized trio of German, Japanese, and Italian soldiers torturing Jesus on the cross is not far different than Gino Boccasile's anti-American poster of a vulgarly illustrated African-American soldier plundering a church as the Christ on the Cross teeters overhead. Both are meant to elicit powerful nationalistic feelings from the viewer, and both use exaggeration and hyperbole to make the case of the enemy as evil, inhuman beings.

Success in both wars came not just from the fighting men on the front but, as importantly, from the efforts of the public back home: family members and factory workers, young and old, new immigrants and old established families. Posters survive as reminders not just of the evil of the war, but also of the good done by all who participated and prevailed: some in the factories and farms, others often at the very price of their own lives.

THE ARTISTS

Posters were created by countless artists—prominent fine and commercial artists, along with unknown amateurs and anonymous draftsmen alike. The artists listed below, with brief biographies, represent just a small selection of those who created posters during the war. Inclusion in this list is based on the number of works created, the prominence of the work, and the importance/impact of the posters.

AMERICAN

Boris Artzybasheff 1899–1965: Russian born American commercial illustrator. Winner of the Newbery Medal (1928) and Caldecott Honor (1938) for children's book illustration. Artzybasheff's series of posters for Wickwire Steel were created with just one requirement from the client: each poster must include a product manufactured by Wickwire. Following WWII, Artzybasheff created commercial art for clients including Xerox and Pan Am.

McClelland Barclay 1891–1943: Commercial artist who provided art for publications including *Collier's*, the *Saturday Evening Post*, *Cosmopolitan*, and numerous others. In addition to illustration art, Barclay created jewelry, decorative arts, and housewares. In 1940, Barclay reported for duty in the US Navy, first serving in the New York recruiting office as an illustrator. After fighting for a chance at active duty, Barclay served in the Atlantic and Pacific and was reported lost at sea in 1943 while on board LST 342, which was torpedoed in the Solomon Islands.

CC (Cecil Calvert) Beall 1892–1967: Commercial artist who created advertising and magazine illustrations for Maxwell House Coffee and *Collier's* magazine. Of the several WWII posters illustrated by Beall, his best known, *7th War Loan Now – All Together*, is an illustration of Joe Rosenthal's iconic photograph *Raising the Flag on Iwo Jima*.

Thomas Hart Benton 1889–1975: Along with Grant Wood and John Steuart Curry, he was one of the three great American Regionalist painters. His highly stylized illustrations are distinctly contrasted by Rockwell's photo illustrative style of real everyday people. Following Pearl Harbor, Benton created six paintings for his *Year of Peril* series and wrote an accompanying essay describing his views on the importance of America's entry into the war.

Jean Carlu 1900–1997: French born Carlu studied to become an architect. Following the loss of his right arm at the age of eighteen in an accident, his work focused on graphic design. His architectural background clearly influences the style of his graphic works: bold lines and geometric shapes with little interest in fully developed illustrations. During WWII, Carlu lived in the United States and created posters predominantly focusing on the home front, production, and security.

Howard Chandler Christy 1873–1952: A commercial illustrator best known for his stylized "Christy Girl." From the Spanish-American War through WWII, Christy's illustrations were used in magazines and propaganda posters.

John Steuart Curry 1897–1946: One of the three great American Regionalist painters alongside Thomas Hart Benton and Grant Wood. His sole WWII poster is *Our Good Earth, ...Keep it Ours*.

Stevan Dohanos 1907–1994: American social realist. Created numerous *Saturday Evening Post* covers. During WWII, Dohanos created several "Careless Talk" posters.

Albert Dorne 1906–1965: An illustration artist, Dorne created work for the *Saturday Evening Post*, *Life*, and *Collier's*. Following WWII, Dorne led a group of artists in the creation of the "Famous Artists School." Among the original 1948 faculty were John Atherton, Steven Dohanos, Norman Rockwell, and Jon Whitcomb—all important artists of WWII posters.

Ess-Ar-Gee (Seymour R. Goff) 1904–1992: Art director at House of Seagram, Ess-Ar-Gee, he created a series of anti-espionage posters for placement in bars and taverns where Seagram's products were sold. Ess-Ar-Gee is frequently misidentified as Henry Sharp Goff, Jr.

John Falter, USNR 1910–1982: Prior to WWII, Falter created commercial and illustration art for magazine and advertising. In 1943, Falter entered the Navy as an enlisted man and rose to the rank of lieutenant on special assignment as an artist. Following the war, Falter created his best known body of work—over 100 *Saturday Evening Post* covers—while also producing art for *Esquire*, *Good Housekeeping*, *Look*, and numerous other publications.

James Montgomery Flagg 1877–1960: A prolific illustrator of cartoons, cover art, and advertisements. Flagg's iconic *I Want YOU!* illustrated in 1917 is arguably the single best known poster ever created.

Vernon Grant 1902–1990: A commercial illustrator best known for creating Rice Krispies' "Snap! Crackle! and Pop!" His cartoon-like and humorous style was used in commercial art for advertising and magazine clients.

E (Edward) McKnight Kauffer 1890–1954: American born Kauffer studied in Paris and moved to London at the start of WWI. Creating hundreds of posters for the London Underground, Shell Oil, and other commercial clients, Kauffer returned to the United States in 1940, at the beginning of WWII, and created posters for the war effort. Following the war and until his death Kauffer created a series of posters for American and Pan American Airlines.

Norman Rockwell 1894–1978: Among the many *Saturday Evening Post* illustrators, Rockwell's numerous covers of "everyday Americans" made him one of the most notable illustrators of the pre-WWII era. Rockwell's *Four Freedoms* posters are possibly the best known of all WWII posters.

Jes Schlaijker 1897–1982: After serving in the US Army in WWI, Schlaijker remained in Paris and studied at the Ecole des Beaux Arts, Lyon. Prior to WWII, his illustration art appeared in mainstream magazines and as cover art for "pulps." In 1942, Schlaijker was commissioned by the War Department to create a series of recruiting posters for the Signal Corps, Infantry, Army Air Force, and other branches of military service.

Ben Shahn 1898–1969: Lithuanian born American polyglot. During the Depression, Shahn assisted Diego Rivera's creation of the Rockefeller Center mural, then worked as a photographer for the Farm Security Administration. Shahn's most noted WWII poster *This is Nazi Brutality* depicts the Nazis reporting the destruction of the Czech town of Lidice. Following WWII, Shahn created countless commercial illustrations and works of fine art.

Edward Steichen 1879–1973: Little known in the area of poster art, Steichen was best known for his work in the field of commercial and fine art photography. During WWII, Steichen served as director of the Naval Aviation Photographic Unit, overseeing the creation of a series of recruiting posters, and directed *The Fighting Lady*, 1945 Academy Award winner for Best Documentary. Following the war, Steichen served as director of photography at the Museum of Modern Art in New York and curated the 1955 exhibit *The Family of Man*.

Adolph Treidler 1886–1981: A fine and commercial artist, Treidler's illustration art was created for magazines including the *Saturday Evening Post*, *Harper's*, *Collier's*, and advertising art for Pierce Arrow and the Bermuda Board of Trade.

Tom B. Woodburn 1893–1980: Art director and editor of *Recruiting News* and head of the Army's Recruiting Publicity Service. Created numerous recruiting posters and cover art for patriotic sheet music. Many of Woodburn's earlier posters are signed "Maj." By 1941, he had been promoted to lieutenant colonel.

NC (Newell Convers) Wyeth 1882–1945: Now known as one of America's greatest fine artists, Wyeth's largest body of works was in the field of commercial illustration for magazines, books, and advertisements.

BRITISH

Fougasse (Cyril Kenneth Bird) 1887–1965: Following serious injury in WWI, Fougasse returned to England and rose to the position of editor of *Punch Magazine* in 1939. Most well known as a cartoonist, he created numerous advertising campaigns and posters using his own simple style of illustration. His series of WWII *Careless Talk* propaganda posters are among the best known British posters of the era.

Abram Games 1914–1996: One of the greatest graphic designers of the twentieth century, Games' strength was in his bold, powerful colors and typographic sensibility. Before and following WWII, Games created advertising and marketing materials, book jackets, postage stamps, magazine covers, and logos. His clients included British Airways, Guinness Beer, Penguin Books, and the countries Israel, Ireland, and Portugal.

Pat Keely 1901–1970: A lesser known graphic designer, prior to WWII Keely worked for clients including the London Underground and Southern Railway. During the war, he created numerous posters for the British Ministry of Information. While less known than other designers of the era, his art deco style was bold and readily accessible to the viewer through its simple graphics and strong visual statements.

Norman Wilkinson 1878–1971: Primarily a fine art marine painter by training and interest, Wilkinson was instrumental in developing camouflage in WWI and WWII. His numerous posters for the London and North Western Railway and the London Midland and Scottish Railway often captured marine subjects, as did his war posters.

Zero (Hans Schleger) 1898–1976: German born Schleger studied art in Berlin before moving first to the United States and later settling in Britain in 1932. While in the United States, Schleger took the pseudonym Zero. He was a leading graphic designer and early proponent of the concept of "corporate identity." Zero's posters frequently include modernist style and the use of photomontage.

AXIS

Gino Boccasile 1901–1952: An Italian born prolific commercial artist and illustrator. Prior to WWII, Boccasile worked under fellow Italian Achille Mauzan, following him to Buenos Aires in the 1920s. After a brief period in Paris, Boccasile returned to Milan, and as a personal supporter of Mussolini, he produced numerous racist and anti-Semitic propaganda posters for the fascist government. Boccasile enlisted in the Italian SS and following the war was tried as a collaborator. Acquitted, he was still unable to find work for several years; by the late 1940s he had opened his own successful agency, again producing posters for corporate clients.

COLLECTING WAR POSTERS: A GUIDE TO THE BASICS

Posters of all genres are viewed by collectors based on a number of criteria: artistry, design, subject, condition, rarity, and more. As in any field, knowledge is the key to making wise choices in building a collection that will make its owner proud and satisfied.

Collecting posters is a passion; collecting military/propaganda posters is a passion with a patriotic bent. Collections can be based on broadly defined categories: branches of service, home front causes, country of origin, graphic imagery, etc. A war poster collection can be exclusively from one world war or include posters from both world wars, the Korean conflict, and the Vietnam War/Cold War. A collection can include just one example each from a variety of categories, or it can focus on a specific field. With a range in prices from well under a hundred to over $10,000, original war posters are accessible to almost all collectors. The enjoyment and appreciation of one's collection need not be based on being able to afford the most expensive pieces.

War posters, like advertising, travel, and other posters, are ephemeral items. They were meant to be used, and were frequently irreversibly glued in locations exposed to the weather. Once a poster was pasted up as intended, in almost all cases it could no longer be saved. The posters that do survive do so for a variety of reasons. For example, libraries put aside specimens, posters were pinned up rather than pasted and were thus removable, or they were saved by recipients as patriotic mementos rather than displayed. Even with these and other reasons, the numbers that survive, while unknown, are not large. Not often, but occasionally, WWII posters include a quantity in the printers' note at the bottom of the poster. These quantities give a clue as to why so few exist. Recruiting posters often had print runs identified. The Army Air Force posters shown in Plates 21–22 each indicate a press run of just 10,000 copies; with this small quantity it is clear few would exist in any condition, let alone in excellent condition. Very rarely were posters printed in quantities greater than 100,000.

By the beginning of WWII, printing technology had shifted almost exclusively from stone lithography to offset lithography, or "4 color process" printing. There are exceptions, as posters were occasionally printed as stone lithos, silkscreens, etc., but the vast majority of the posters printed during WWII are offset.

Standardized poster grading uses a letter scale from A to D:

Condition A: A poster in very fine condition with original unfaded colors and no paper loss. There may be small edge tear(s), but nothing significant or impacting the body of the poster. A+ would describe a perfect example, which is exceedingly rare. An A- poster may have slight surface dirt or minor restoration that should be unobtrusive.

Condition B: A poster in good condition with minor paper loss at the edges, but not in any significant amount, nor in a crucial area of the graphic. Any restoration should have been professionally done and not immediately visible to the naked eye. Any fading, color loss, or toning to the paper (light staining) should be very minor and not affect the overall look of the poster. B+ indicates a poster in very good condition. B- would indicate slightly more of the issues described.

Condition C: A poster in fair condition with obvious fading or staining, some missing paper, and tears. Fading should not be so significant as to change the overall look of the poster. Restoration may be immediately evident.

Condition D: A poster in poor or worse condition. Missing significant paper, faded, or light burned so as to make the original artist's vision difficult or impossible to see.

The condition is based on an unrestored viewing of a poster and does *not* improve as a result of restoration. While restoration to tears and losses or overpainting to restore lost/faded color may result in a pleasing visual, it does not alter the underlying condition of the poster.

The descriptions above do not include mention of fold lines. When a poster was machine folded for original distribution, residual fold line remnants are not damage, nor do they harm the value of a poster. When fold lines occur after the fact as the result of an unfolded poster being folded they would be considered damage, and would affect the condition and value. Most US government issued posters of WWII were originally folded for mailing.

Linen backing will greatly mitigate these fold lines, often making them all but invisible. This backing process is the industry standard of conservation. A piece of canvas is stretched as if for a painting. Acid free barrier paper is laid down and then the poster is pasted on the acid free paper. All is done using an acid free wheat paste. This process is fully reversible and gives support to the poster. Dry mounting should *never* be used, as this process is irreversible and the dry mount film, mounting board, and poster all expand and contract at different rates with changes in temperature and humidity. This can cause significant and uncorrectable damage to a poster. Framing a poster should be done by a framer experienced with this media and sized artwork. Ultraviolet protection is an absolute necessity and UV Plexiglas is recommended. Due to degradation of the material, the common current practice is to replace the Plexiglas approximately every twenty years.

A collector should strive to buy a poster in the best condition available. Common WWII posters are frequently found in A and B condition, and only rarely should a C be considered. An exceedingly rare piece which may never be seen again might be purchased in a lesser condition with the hope of someday replacing it with a better example. With this in mind, the change in value of a poster based on the condition is more impacted for a common, lower-value poster than for a rare and desirable piece. Only under extraordinary conditions should one consider a D condition poster.

Each government had a standardized series of sizes, and basic print sheets were as follows (in inches):

United States

¼ sheet	10 × 14
½ sheet	20 × 28
1 sheet	28 × 40
2 sheet	40 × 56

United Kingdom

¼ sheet	10 × 15
½ sheet	15 × 20
Double Crown	20 × 30
Quad or Quad Crown	30 × 40
Double Royal	25 × 40
Double Quad	40 × 60

France

½ sheet	31½ × 47 (80 × 120 cm)
1 sheet	47 × 63 (120 × 160 cm)

Italy

Un-Foglio	27 × 30 (70 × 100 cm)
Due-Foglio	39 × 55 (100 × 140 cm)
Quattro-Foglio	55 × 78 (140 × 200 cm)

These sizes are quite variable, and many posters were printed in multiple sizes. Some posters, including N C Wyeth's *Buy War Bonds* (Plate 111), were printed in more than six sizes

(variations 11 × 14, 14 × 22, 20 × 28, 28 × 40, 30 × 40, and 40 × 60). Frequently, branches of service would have a standard size different than those cited above. Smaller posters were often issued on card stock, some with easel backs for quick and easy display.

Privately printed posters frequently matched the clients' existing poster program. For example, before and after the war, New Haven Railroad travel and advertising posters were 28 × 42 in., and during the war NHRR propaganda posters (Plates 340–345) were the same size, presumably to fit into existing display locations.

As propaganda and war posters are so significant in the history of nations, many libraries, museums, and other national institutions maintain vast and wonderful collections. Each institution may have on display only such pieces that are of significance to a current exhibit or show, but their collections will also frequently include a larger range of material. Some institutions will offer access to additional pieces not on active display by appointment. Many of these collections are now also viewable online. Among the most significant collections are held by the following:

United States Library of Congress (loc.gov)
Imperial War Museum (iwm.org.uk)
Smithsonian Institution (si.edu)
Museum of Modern Art (moma.org)
Bibliotheque Nationale de France (bnf.fr)
Bibliotheque Nationale de Quebec (banq.qc.ca)
Canadian War Museum (*Musee Canadien de la Guerre*- warmuseum.ca)

Countless historical societies, corporations, libraries, and colleges and universities hold smaller collections, often with rare and interesting posters specific to their local region or economy. These collections are also frequently accessible online. Research institutions with digitally accessible collections include:

Northwestern University Library (https://images.northwestern. edu/
University of Washington Library (http://content.lib.washington. edu/postersweb/)
McGill Digital Library (http://digital.library.mcgill.ca/warposters/)
Harry S. Truman Library and Museum (http://www.trumanlibrary. org/museum/posters/index.html)

The question of "fakes" and "repros" (reproductions) has become a major issue in the field of posters. There are numerous sources for reproductions and digital copies are available on endless web sites. These are of no monetary value, and in almost no cases do they have the visual impact of the original. As copies of the originals, they are rarely full-sized, with the color and clarity seen in the original almost always significantly impaired.

Online public auction sites contain numerous listings of war posters; many are identified as copies or reproductions, and many are unidentified as to date of creation. The vast number of sellers are probably well intended, but lack the specific knowledge necessary to determine the authenticity and accurately describe the condition. Photos frequently offer a lack of detail, and it is impossible to see if the color is faded or the paper is light stained (yellowed). Countless clients have related tales of unmentioned damage, tape slathered on the back of posters, dry mounted posters, poor packing resulting in total loss, etc. The Internet is a wonderful place, but also an unregulated market—never has the expression *caveat emptor* been so apt.

On the other hand, legitimate dealers and professional auction houses will guarantee everything they sell as to authenticity and condition described. For an expensive poster, any restoration should be clearly noted. When restoration is extensive, a "before photo" will frequently be available for viewing.

One of the most important added values of buying from a professional dealer is their knowledge base and access to references that will provide confidence in what is being purchased. When starting out buying lesser priced items, a collector should take advantage of dealer's guidance to "learn the ropes." Then, as a collection grows it is more and more important to work with an experienced dealer to build a coherent collection, choosing pieces that will complement and diversify one's collection. Additionally, when buying expensive pieces, it is most certainly of value to rely on the reputation and resources of an expert.

One should enjoy the process of building a collection and the experience of seeing one's posters regularly. A great collection is one that is enjoyed by its owner. A collection can be just a handful of pieces framed and looked at daily or a vast trove of posters built over years and studied and contemplated for hours on end. The importance is the meaningfulness to the collector.

Plates 2-5, United States Army Recruiting
1942, 19 × 25

Plate 6, Defend Your Country, Enlist Now
1940, 25 × 38 *

Plate 7, U.S. Army, Guardian of the Colors
1940, 25 × 38 *

Plate 8, U.S. Army, At Home Abroad
1940, 25 × 38

Plate 9, Defend Your Country, Enlist Now
1940, 59 × 46

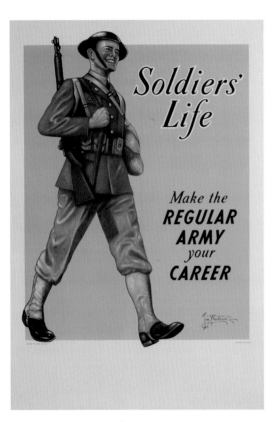

Plate 10, Soldiers' Life
1941, 25 × 38

Plate 11, Remain with the Colors
1938, 9 × 13

Plate 12, Don't Gamble with Your Future
1946, 25 × 38

Plate 13, I Want You for the U.S. Army
1941, 9 × 12½ *

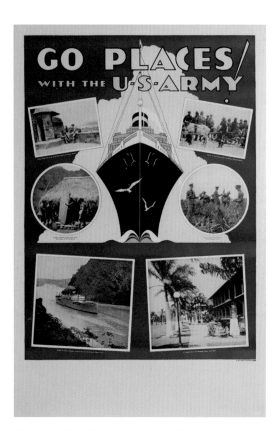

Plate 14, Go Places with the U.S. Army
1940, 25 × 38

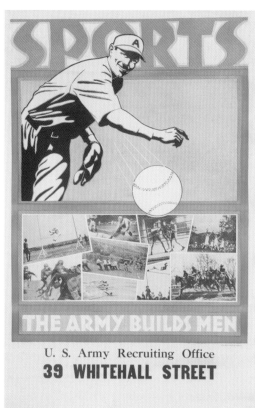

Plate 15, Sports, the Army Builds Men,
1937, 25 × 38

Plate 16, Vacancies Exist! Enlist Now, U.S. Army
1939, 25 × 38

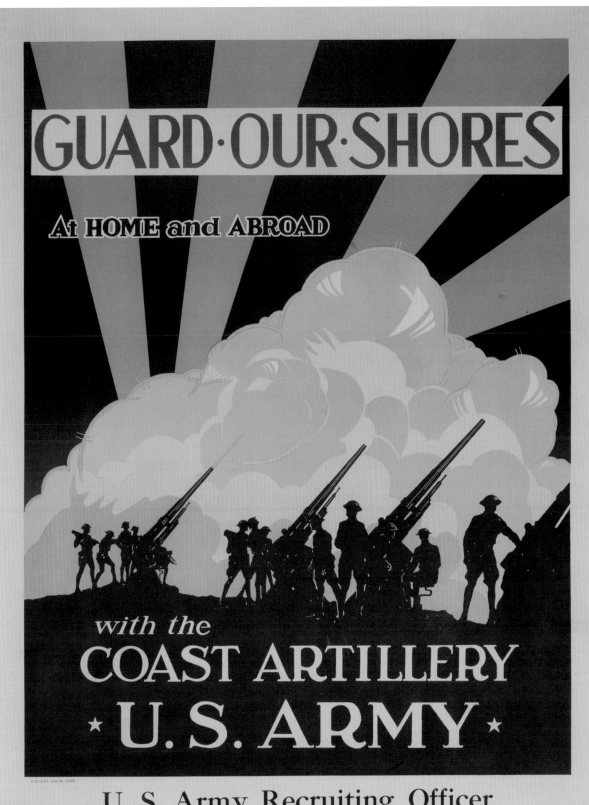

Plate 17, Guard Our Shores, U.S. Army
1940, 25 × 38

Plate 18, West Point of the Air—Flying Cadets
1940, 25 × 38

Plate 19, West Point of the Air—Flying Cadets
1939, 25 × 38

Plates 20-22, AAF — Greatest Team in the World
1944, 25 × 38

Plate 23, Wings Over America
1940, 25 × 38

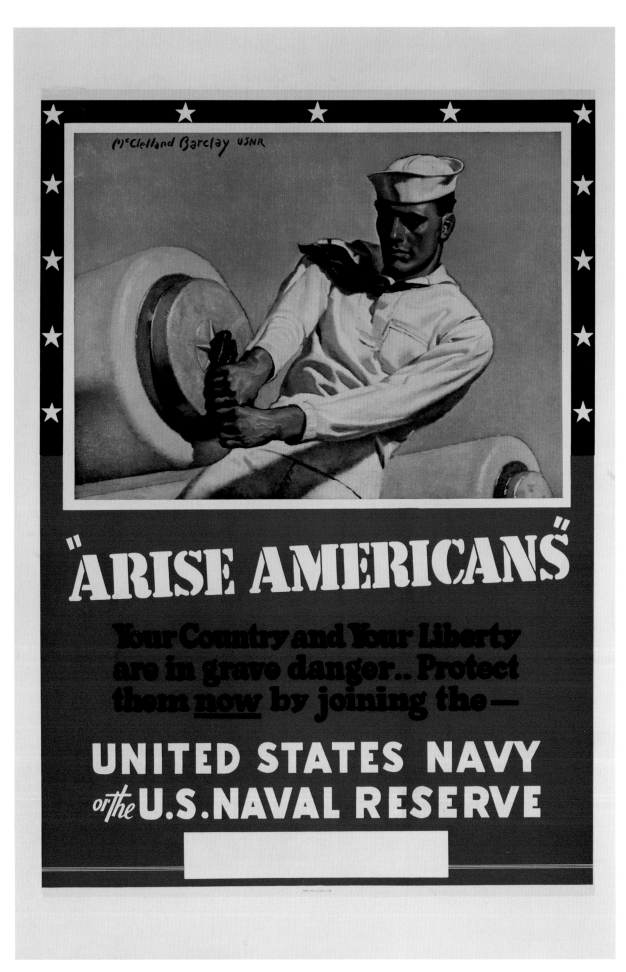

Plate 24, Arise Americans, United States Navy
1941, 27 × 41

Plate 25, Protect Your Future, Learn a Trade
1941, 21 × 11

Plate 26, Fighting Fish and Fighting Men
1941, 20 × 14

Plate 27, Fight, Let's Go! Join the Navy
1942, 20 × 14

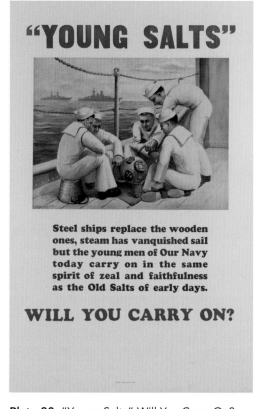

Plate 28, Contact!
1935, 28 × 42

Plate 29, Join the Navy and Free the World
1942, 28 × 42

Plate 30, "Young Salts" Will You Carry On?
1934, 27 × 42

Plate 31, Dish It Out with the Navy!
1942, 28 × 41

Plate 32, Naval Aviation Has a Place for You
ca. 1942, 28 × 41

Plate 33, Spearhead of Victory, Navy Day
1943, 26 × 37½

NAVY BLIMPS   K-ships leave their hangar for Atlantic submarine patrol.

Plates 34-35, Aviation Training Division
ca. 1942, 39 × 59

ECHELON — AVENGERS

Looking like angry hornets, a formation of Navy torpedo bombers roar through the skies.

Plates 36-39, Aviation Training Division
ca. 1942, 39 × 59

BABY FLAT-TOP   Dusk descends on a Navy escort carrier and her brood of sub-scourging
                 Wildcats and Avengers.

YOUR JOB IN THE NAVY
HOW TO TELL IT! WHAT IT MEANS!

Specialty marks on Navy rating badges identify almost fifty different kinds of trade experts trained in the fleet and in Navy trade schools. Here's how to recognize them! Here's what their duties are! Here's what your civilian job can be after the war, if you join the Navy now! Find the rating you like ... then enlist and start Navy training in that trade. If you're already skilled, you may get a rating immediately upon enlistment!

BOATSWAIN'S MATE · · ·
DUTIES: Do canvas and tackle work. Understand navigation and rules of the road. Handle power and sail boats. Understand salvage operation and damage control.
RELATED CIVIL JOBS: Rigger Foreman, Sailor, Hand Operator.

GUNNER'S MATE · · ·
DUTIES: Supervise all phases of gunnery. Know how to handle ammunition. Test smokeless powder. Understand fire control. Handle mines, depth charges, and torpedoes.
RELATED CIVIL JOBS: Gunsmith, Mechanic.

TURRET CAPTAIN · · ·
DUTIES: Take charge of gun turrets and crews. Know guns and gunnery units. Operate directric scopes, periscopes and rangefinders. Understand principles of hydraulics.
RELATED CIVIL JOBS: Skilled Mechanic, Gunsmith.

TORPEDOMAN · · ·
DUTIES: Repair, care and operation of torpedoes and torpedo firing mechanisms. Understand care and operation of gyro compasses. Knowledge of Navy pyrotechnics, principles of mines and depth charges.
RELATED CIVIL JOBS: Skilled Mechanic, Gunsmith.

QUARTERMASTER · · ·
DUTIES: Understand practical application of celestial navigation and dead reckoning. Take soundings and plot bearings. Know care, operation and general maintenance of navigational instruments. Knowledge of visual communication. Thorough knowledge of rules of the road, military honors and ceremonies.
RELATED CIVIL JOBS: Navigator, Ship Pilot, Hydrographer.

SIGNALMAN · · ·
DUTIES: Thorough knowledge of visual communication procedures and instruments. Identification of foreign flags and ensigns. Know rules of the road, military honors and ceremonies.
RELATED CIVIL JOBS: Merchant Marine Quartermaster and Third Mate.

FIRE CONTROLMAN · · ·
DUTIES: Thorough knowledge of electricity. Assembly, inspection and repair of optical instruments used in controlling ship's gun fire. Operation of all fire control instruments. Understand range, deflection, and ballistics.
RELATED CIVIL JOBS: Electrician, Instrument Maker, Optical Repairman.

COOK OR BAKER · · ·
DUTIES: All types of quantity cooking. Steam and range cooking. Bakers must handle bread and pastry processes throughout. Cooks must have knowledge of baking.
RELATED CIVIL JOBS: Chef, Baker, Commissary Manager.

AVIATION MACHINIST'S MATE
DUTIES: Repair and maintenance of aircraft, aircraft engines and instruments. Know theory of aerodynamics and aircraft nomenclature.
RELATED CIVIL JOBS: Aircraft Instrument Repairman, Aircraft Engine Mechanic, Maintenance Man.

AVIATION ORDNANCEMAN
DUTIES: Understand principles of bombs, bomb fuses, bomb sights, aircraft torpedoes, machine guns, their operation, maintenance and repair.
RELATED CIVIL JOBS: Gunsmith, Electrician, Instrument Maker.

ELECTRICIAN'S MATE · · ·
DUTIES: Thorough knowledge of principles and practice of electricity. Wire and repair circuits. Care and operation of high power searchlights. Understand construction and maintenance of A.C. and D.C. motors, generators, and transformers. Gyro compass assembly, repair and operation. Operate, maintain and repair sound motion picture projection equipment. Repair, maintenance and installation of telephone systems.
RELATED CIVIL JOBS: Electrician, Telephone Mechanic, Motion Picture Projectionist.

WATERTENDER OR BOILERMAKER
DUTIES: Operate, repair, and maintain boiler systems. Understand principles of steam engineering, boilers, steamfitting, condensers, evaporators, feed water pipes, and blowers. Know ignition and lubrication.
RELATED CIVIL JOBS: Boiler operator, Boiler inspector, Steamfitter, Plumber, Fireman on railroad or power plant, Stationary Engineer.

SHIPFITTER, BLACKSMITH, METALSMITH, MOULDER · · ·
DUTIES: Bend, repair and fit all pipes and tubing aboard ship. Lay out and accomplish sheet metal projects. Be able to forge, weld and solder all metals used aboard ship. Understand principles of electrical refrigeration, heating and air conditioning. Deep sea diving. Know the characteristics of metals and have a practical knowledge of moulding.
RELATED CIVIL JOBS: Steamfitter, Plumber, Pipefitter, Shipwright, Metal Worker, Welder, Refrigerator Service and Repair Man, Blacksmith, Moulder.

YEOMAN · · ·
DUTIES: Manage ship's offices. Secretarial work. Personnel accounting.
RELATED CIVIL JOBS: Office Manager, Secretary.

AEROGRAPHER
DUTIES: Make weather observations. Draw accurate synoptic weather charts. Install, operate and maintain meteorological observations afloat or ashore. Compare balloon soundings. Understand weather codes.
RELATED CIVIL JOBS: Meteorologist, Aerologist.

AVIATION METALSMITH
DUTIES: Repair and maintenance of aircraft metal work such as plating, pipe connections, instrument castings, and cowlings. Forge, braze, weld, breed, and electroplate all metals used in aircraft. Operate related hand and power tools.
RELATED CIVIL JOBS: Metalsmith, Aviation Metalsmith, Shipfitter, Tinsmith, Plumber, Aircraft Maintenance Man.

AVIATION RADIOMAN
DUTIES: Operation, repair and maintenance of aircraft radio transmitting and receiving equipment. Make frequency adjustments. Operate, repair and calibrate radio direction finders. Encipher and decipher codes.
RELATED CIVIL JOBS: Radioman, Radio Repair Man, Radio Engineer, Flight Radio Operator.

MACHINIST'S MATE · · ·
DUTIES: Operation, maintenance and repair of main and auxiliary engines aboard ship. Operate, maintain and repair drainage systems, distilling plants, internal combustion engines of compression and spark ignition types. Operate machine shop equipment.
RELATED CIVIL JOBS: Machinist, Garage Repairman, Engine Mechanic, Power Plant Engineer, Marine or Stationary Engineer.

CARPENTER'S MATE, PAINTER PATTERNMAKER · · ·
DUTIES: Repair by hand and power tools all woodwork. Know construction of various types of small boats. Know woods used in shipboard construction and equipment. Know their approved uses and how to join and finish them. Have experience in practical patternmaking. Know the characteristics and uses of all paints and varnishes.
RELATED CIVIL JOBS: Carpenter, Ship's Carpenter, Boat Builder, Shipwright, Patternmaker, Cabinet Maker, Painter.

STOREKEEPER · · ·
DUTIES: Payroll accounting. Disbursing. Stock records, stowage and procurement.
RELATED CIVIL JOBS: Stockman, Freight Clerk, Warehouse Record Clerk, Payroll Clerk.

PHARMACIST'S MATE · · ·
DUTIES: Manage ship's sick quarters. Administer simple medicines and anesthesia. Perform minor surgery and first aid. Understand hygiene and sanitation. Thorough knowledge of human anatomy, standard medicines and drugs.
RELATED CIVIL JOBS: Pharmacist, Male Nurse, Hospital Attendant, First Aid Instructor.

MOTOR MACHINIST'S MATE · · ·
DUTIES: Know theory, operation, maintenance and repair of Diesel and gasoline engines. Knowledge of lathe and machine shop work.
RELATED CIVIL JOBS: Diesel Engine Operator and Repairman, Machinist, Automotive Engineer.

RADIOMAN · · ·
DUTIES: Operation, maintenance and repair of Navy radio transmitting and receiving equipment. Make frequency adjustments. Encipher and decipher codes. Understand maintenance, operation, maintenance and repair of sonic depth finding equipment. Motion picture sound equipment operator.
RELATED CIVIL JOBS: Radio Electrician, Licensed Radio Operator or Telegrapher, Sound Technician.

PRINTER · · ·
DUTIES: Set type. Operate linotype and various types of presses. Distinguish type faces, printer's marks, inks, and paper grades. Understand make-up, color composition, electrotyping, lithography, and wood cuts.
RELATED CIVIL JOBS: Printer, Compositor, Linotype Operator, Pressman, Proof Reader.

PHOTOGRAPHER · · ·
DUTIES: General photographic work. Install and operate aerial cameras. Make and assemble aerial mapping photographs. Operate still and motion picture cameras. Photographic processing, still and motion picture. Make up and edit motion picture productions. Manage photographic laboratories ashore and afloat.
RELATED CIVIL JOBS: Photographer, Still or Motion Picture, Motion Picture Projectionist, Aerial Map Maker, Photographic Laboratory Technician.

COMMISSARY STEWARD · · ·
DUTIES: Manage ship's galleys. Plan menus. Estimate quantities of food needed. Direct stowage, refrigeration, and preparation of food. Manage field kitchens for forces operating ashore. Understand seasonal fluctuations of food markets.
RELATED CIVIL JOBS: Restaurant, Cafeteria or Club Commissary Manager, Chef, Baker.

MUSICIAN · · ·
DUTIES: Understand use, care, and handling of at least one band instrument. Read band music or sight. Understand basic principles of harmony. Be able to direct band and assist in manual instruction. Thorough knowledge of musical aspects of military honors and ceremonies.
RELATED CIVIL JOBS: Musician.

BUGLER, BUGLEMASTER · · ·
DUTIES: Sound all bugle and drum calls of daily routine and emergencies, afloat and ashore. Be familiar with honors rendered and the etiquette of the side and quarter deck. Know the marches used in the Navy.
RELATED CIVIL JOBS: Musician, Bugler, Buglemaster.

The Navy has recently authorized the following new ratings:
PARACHUTE RIGGER, RADARMAN, SOUNDMAN, AVIATION PILOT AND RADIO TECHNICIAN.

Enlist IN THE NAVY *today!*

NRB—72695—4-16-42—25M

Plate 40, Your Job in the Navy
1942, 28 × 42

Plate 41, "Sub Spotted—Let 'Em Have It!"
ca. 1942, 28 × 42

Plate 42, Let's Hit 'Em with Everything
1942, 28 × 42

Plate 43, The United States Navy Needs...
1940, 28 × 42

Plate 44, Keep it Great! Become a Naval Officer
1942, 28 × 42

Plate 45, Enemy Sighted—Attack!
1942, 28 × 42

Plate 46, Train Today, Submarine Service
1944, 18 × 24

Plate 47, Smack the Japs!
1944, 22 × 28

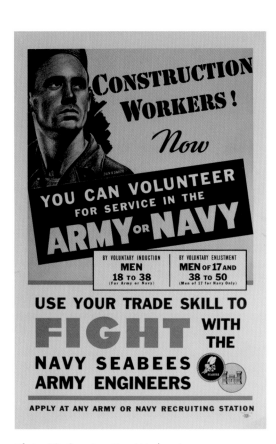

Plate 48, Construction Workers!
1943, 25 × 38

Plate 49, Build for Your Navy!
ca. 1942, 14 × 22

Plate 50, Construction Workers!
1943, 25 × 38

Plate 51, Join the Seabees
1943, 14 × 22 *

Plate 52, The U.S. Marines Want You
1942, 14 × 22

Plate 53, Ready, Join U.S. Marines
1942, 28 × 40

Plate 54, On to Victory, U.S. Marines
1942, 11 × 14

Plate 55, Fly with the Marines
1942, 28 × 40

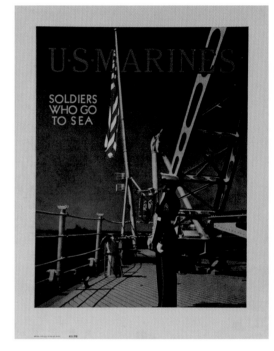

Plate 56, U.S. Marines, Soldiers Who Go to Sea
1942, 11 × 14

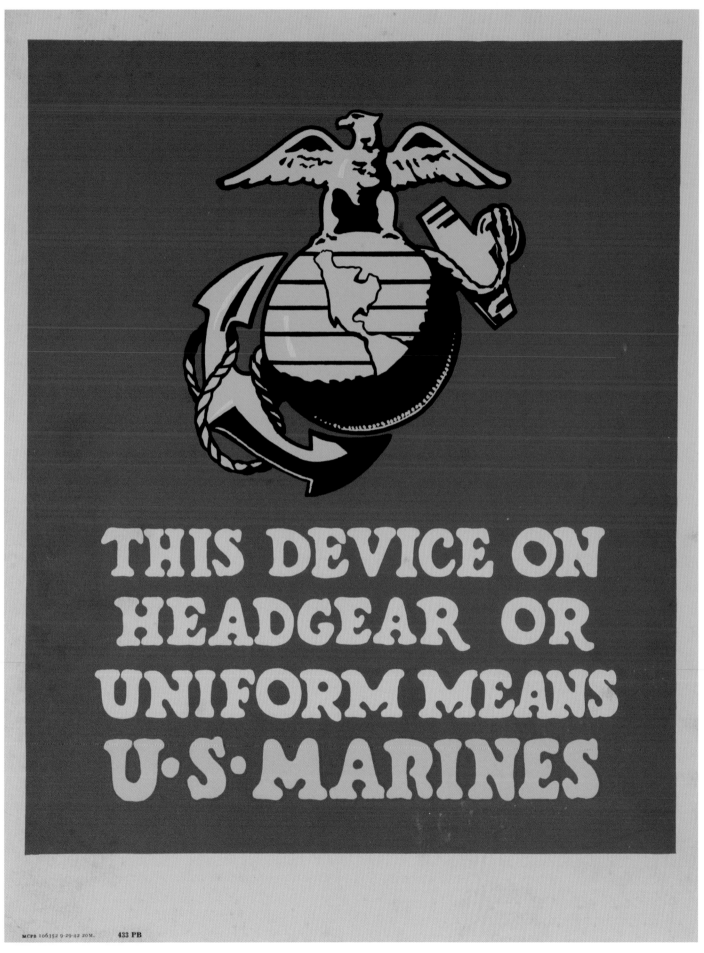

Plate 57, This Device Means U. S. Marines
1942, 11 × 14

Plate 58, U.S. Marines Deliver the Goods Too
1942, 58½ × 45½

Plate 59, Land with the U. S. Marines
1942, 28 × 40

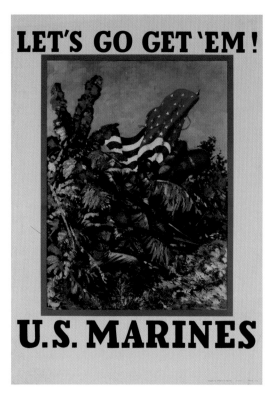

Plate 60, Let's Go Get 'Em! U.S. Marines
1942, 11 × 14 *

Plate 61, Hit Hard and Often, with the Marines
1942, 11 × 14 *

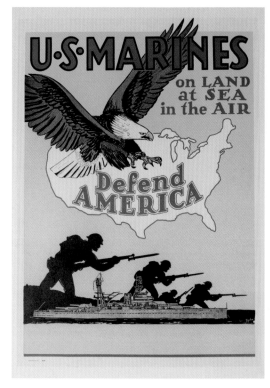

Plate 62, U.S. Marines, Defend America
1941, 30 × 40

Plate 63, Always Advance with the U.S. Marines
1942, 28 × 22

Plate 64, "The Marines Have Landed!"
1942, 30 × 40

Plate 65, Want Action? Join U.S. Marines Corps!
1942, 30 × 40

Plate 66, Always Ready, U.S. Coast Guard
ca. 1942, 22 × 28

Plate 67, Clear for Action, U.S. Coast Guard
1943, 28 × 42

Plate 68, Every Minute Counts
ca. 1942, 22 × 28

Plates 69 & 70, U.S. Coast Guard
Blast 'Em 1943 & Defend 1941, 21 × 11

Plate 71, On Watch! U.S. Coast Guard
1943, 14 × 19

Plate 72, Good Hunting with the U.S. Coast Guard
1943, 14 × 19

Plate 73, Go Higher, U.S. Air Force
1948, 24 × 37

Plate 74, A Career in the Air, U.S. Air Force
1948, 24 × 36

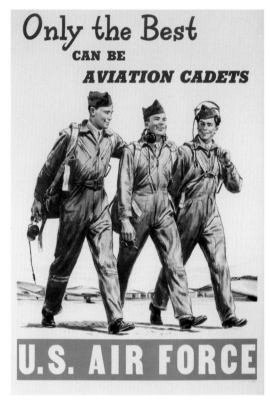

Plate 75, Only the Best, U.S. Air Force
1948, 24 × 36

Plate 76, U.S. Air Force, Air Power Is Peace Power
1948, 25 × 38

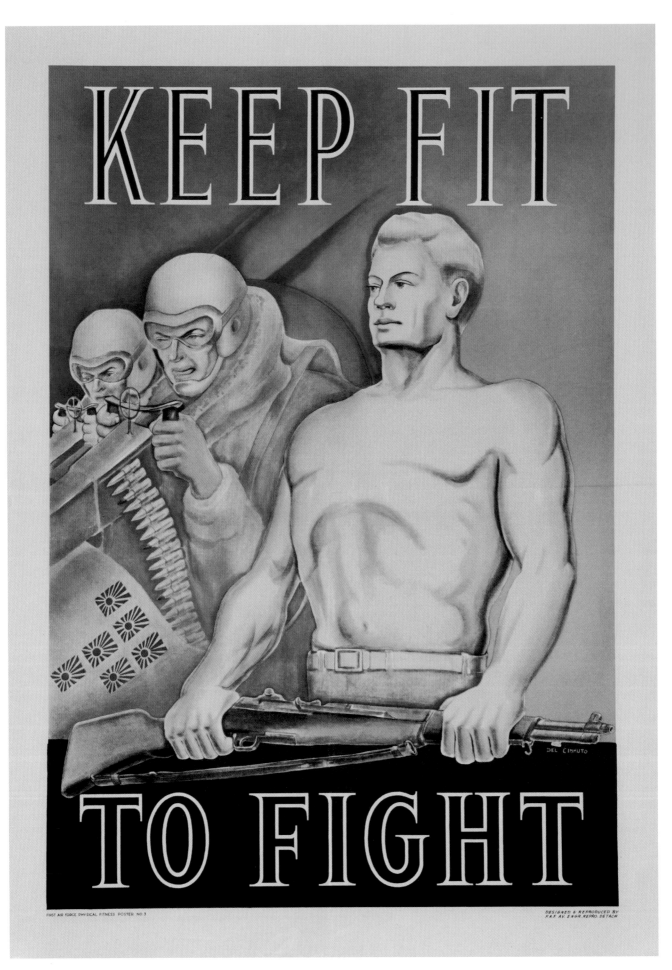

Plate 77, Keep Fit to Fight
ca. 1942, 14 × 19½

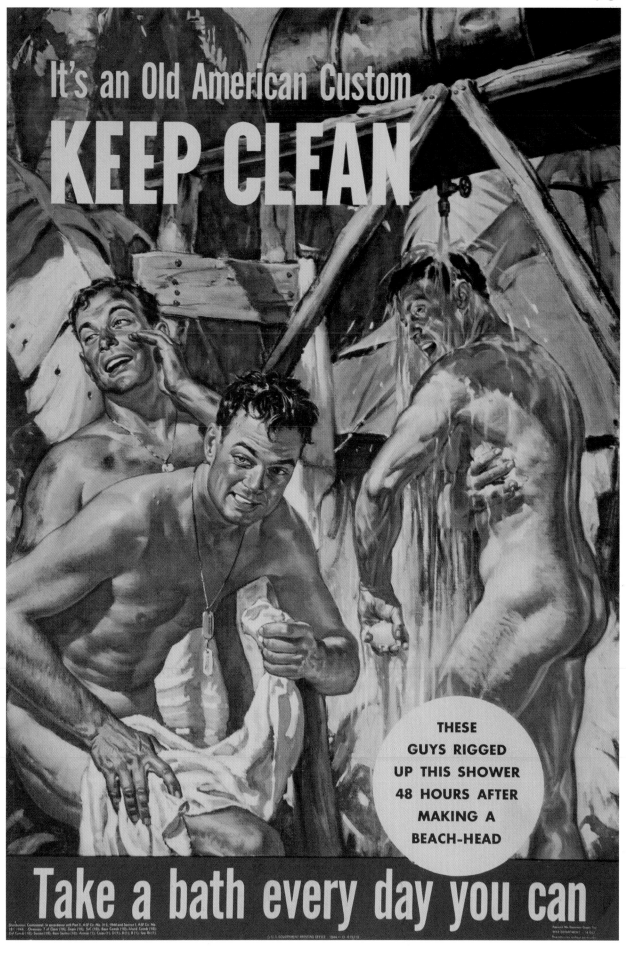

Plate 78, Keep Clean, Take a Bath Every Day
ca. 1944, 14 × 20

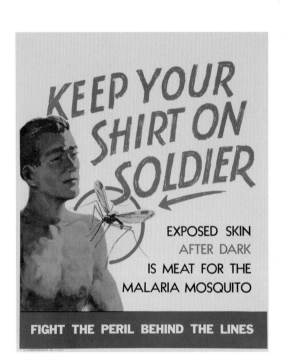

Plate 79, Keep Your Shirt on Soldier
1943, 14 × 17

Plate 80, Don't Let Lice Make a Monkey out of You!
1944, 14 × 20

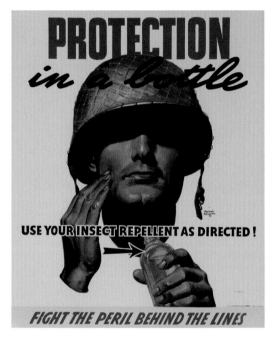

Plate 81, Protection in a Bottle
1944, 14 × 17

Plate 82, Net Profit, Avoid Malaria
1946, 13 × 18½

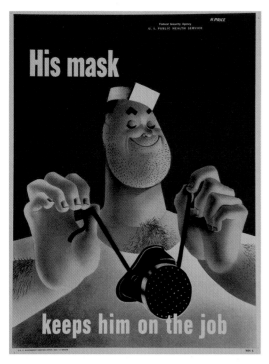
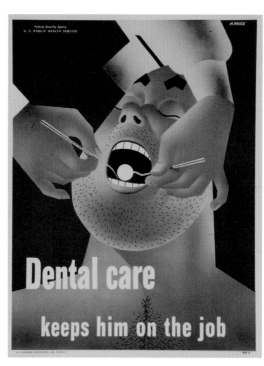

Plates 83-89, Keep Him on the Job
1942, 9½ × 12½

Federal Security Agency
U. S. PUBLIC HEALTH SERVICE

H.PRICE

Regular check ups keep him on the job

☆ U. S. GOVERNMENT PRINTING OFFICE: 1942—O-460435

WH 7

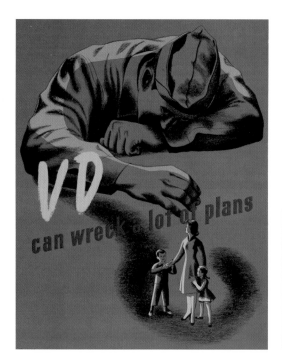

Plate 90, VD Can Wreck a Lot of Plans
ca. 1945, 15 × 20

Plate 91, Syphilis, a Million New Victims Each
Year ca. 1942, 15 × 20

Plate 92, Go Back to Civvies Clean
ca. 1944,15 × 20

Plate 93, VD, a Sorry Ending to a Furlough
ca. 1942, 16 × 21

Plate 94, The New Pro Kit
ca. 1942, 11 × 14

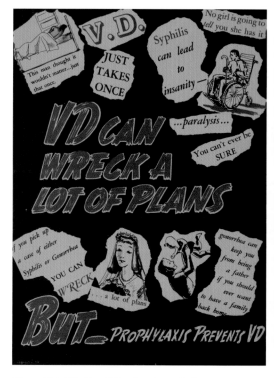

Plate 95, VD Can Wreck a Lot of Plans
ca. 1942, 16 × 19

Plate 96, VD May Ruin Your Career
ca. 1942, 15 × 20

Plate 97, Furlough "Booby Trap!"
ca. 1944, 14 × 18

Plate 98, There's Nothing New Under the Sun
1946, 18 × 26

Plate 99, There's No Medicine for Regret
1945, 18½ × 25½

Plate 100, If You Must be a Dumb Bunny...
1945, 18½ × 25½

Plate 101, Juke Joint Sniper
ca. 1944, 15 × 20

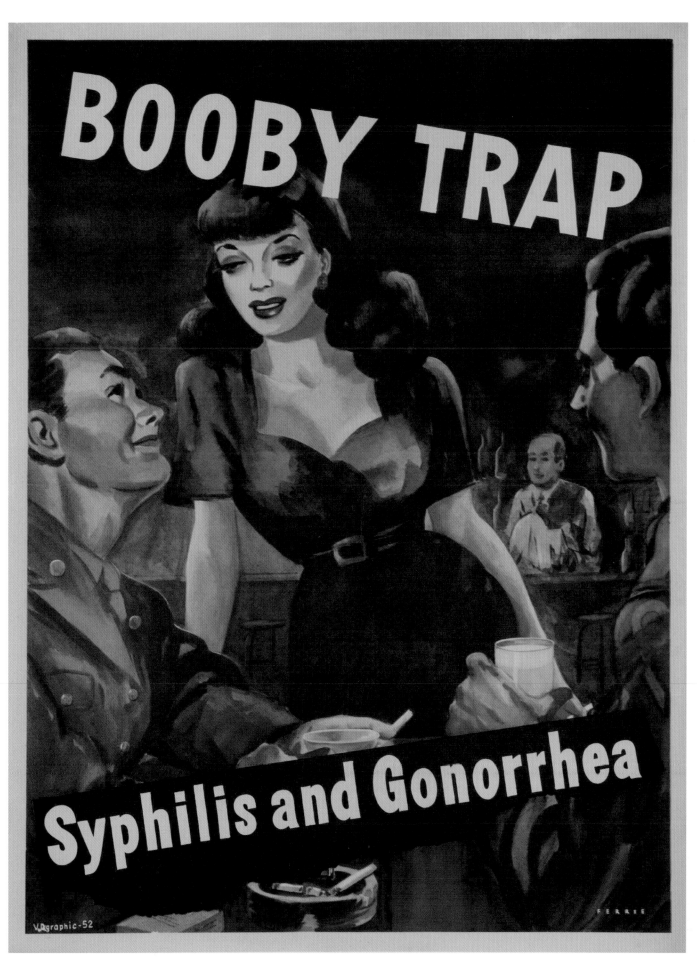

Plate 102, Booby Trap
ca. 1944, 15 × 20

Plate 103, An Enemy Still to be Defeated, VD
ca. 1945, 60 × 46

Plate 104, Most Promiscuous Women Have VD
1944, 14 × 22

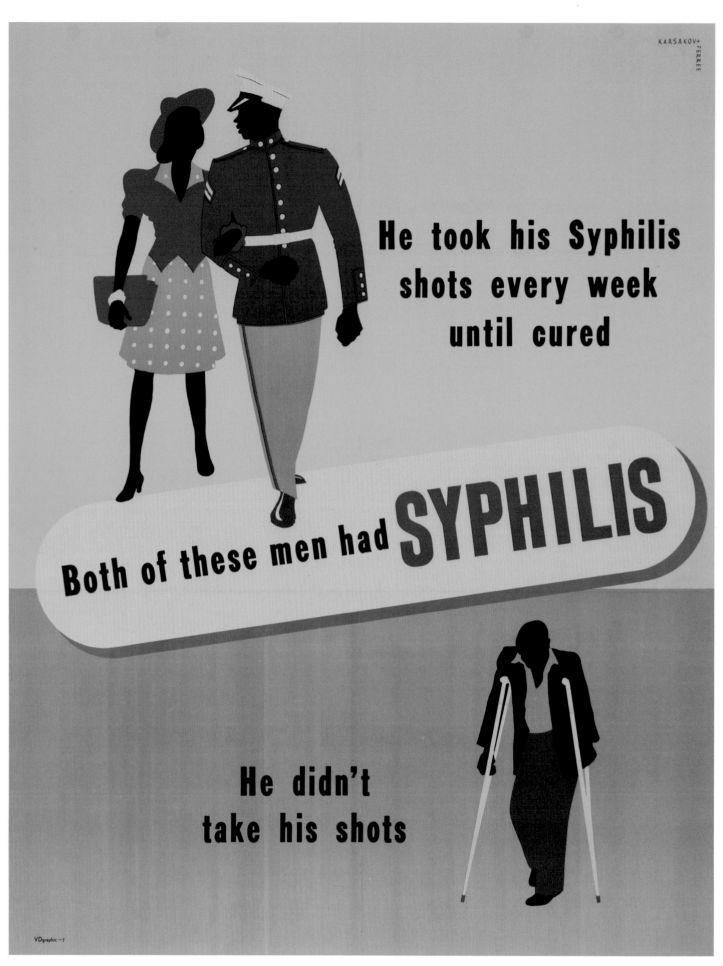

Plate 105, Both of These Men Had Syphilis
ca. 1941, 20 × 28

Plate 106, Venereal Disease Covers the Earth
ca. 1942, 15 × 25

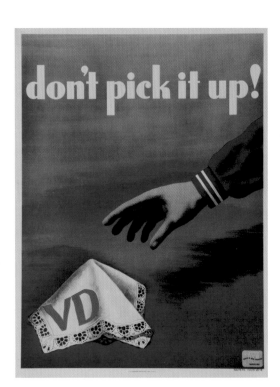

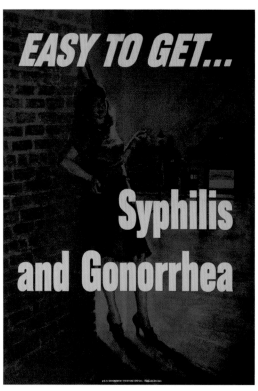

Plate 107, Don't Pick it Up! VD
1948, 15 × 25

Plate 108, Easy to Get ... Syphilis and Gonorrhea
ca. 1943, 14 × 20

Plate 109, Easy to Get ... Syphilis and Gonorrhea
1943, 14 × 22

Plate 110, Bright Future Ahead, Steer Clear of VD
1948, 14 × 18

Plate 111, Buy War Bonds
1942, 30 × 40 *

Plate 112, Our Good Earth ... Keep it Ours
1942, 40 × 60 *

Plate 113, Buy a Share in America
1941, 40½ × 56 *

Plate 114, Hasten the Homecoming
ca. 1945, 20 × 29

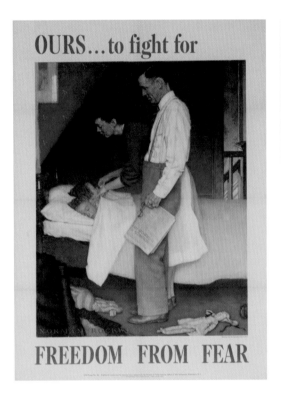

Plates 115-118, The Four Freedoms
1943, 20 × 28 *

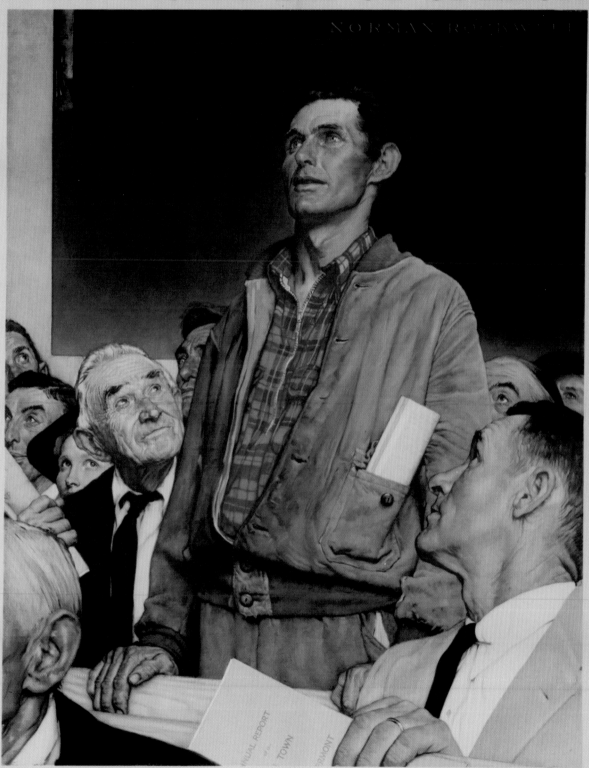

Plate 119, Don't Let That Shadow Touch Them
1942, 28 × 40

Plate 120, Deliver Us from Evil
1943, 20 × 28 *

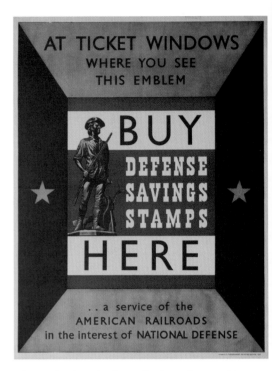

Plate 121, Buy Defense Savings Stamps Here
1941, 22 × 28

Plate 122, Let's Fly This Flag, 10% in War Bonds
1942, 22 × 28

Plate 123, For Victory ...
1942, 17 × 22

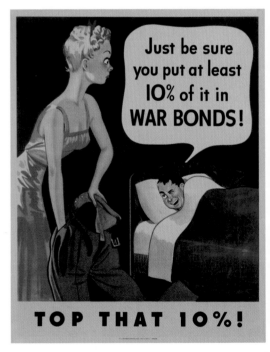

Plate 124,Top That 10%
1942, 22 × 28

Plate 125, Attack Attack Attack, Buy War Bonds
1942, 28 × 40 *

Plate 126, "You Buy 'Em, We'll Fly 'Em!"
1942, 20 × 28 *

Plate 127, Till We Meet Again, Buy War Bonds
1942, 16 × 22 *

Plate 128, For Their Future—Buy War Bonds
1943, 28 × 40

Plate 129, "Even a Little Can Help a Lot—Now"
1942, 14 × 20

Plate 130, We Can ... We Will ... We Must!
1942, 20½ × 11

Plate 131, Buy That Invasion Bond!
1944, 40 × 28

Plate 132, Jap ... You're Next! Buy Extra Bonds
1944, 20 × 28 *

Plate 133, 7th War Loan, Now—All Together
1945, 26 × 37 *

Plate 134, Women's Army Corps
1944, 20 × 28

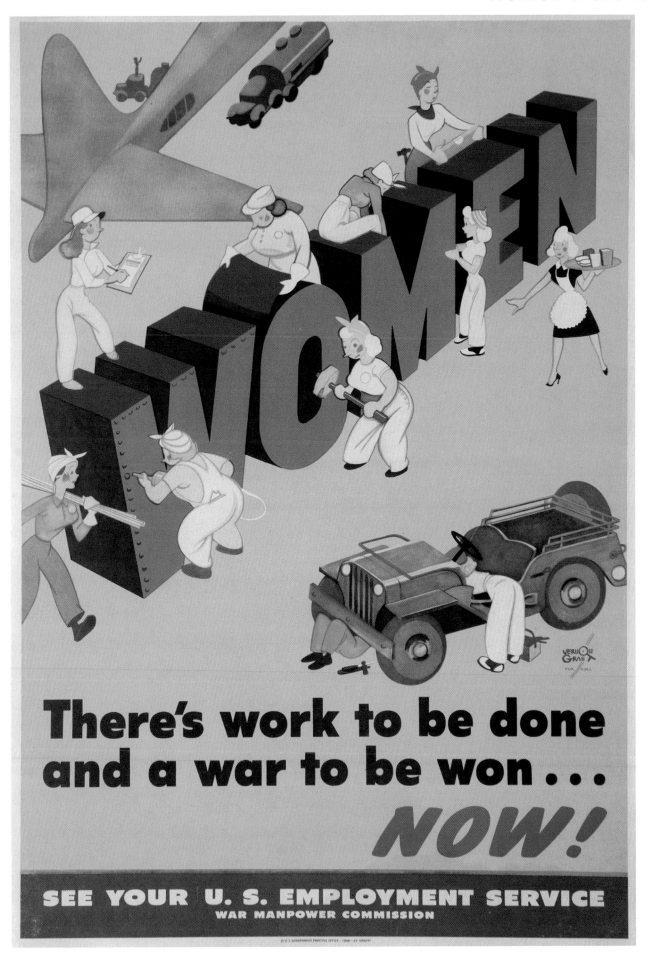

Plate 135, Women There's Work to Be Done
1944, 14 × 20 *

Plate 136, "The Girl He Left Behind" She's a WOW
1943, 27 × 42

Plate 137, She's a WOW
1942, 27 × 42

Plate 138, Enlist in a Proud Profession!
ca. 1942, 20 × 28

Plate 139, Join the Army Nurse Corp
1943, 20½ × 31

Plate 140, Enlist in a Proud Profession ...
1943, 20 × 28

Plate 141, Become a Nurse, Your Country Needs You
1942, 20 × 28 *

Plate 142, Enlist in the WAVES
1943, 28 × 42

Plate 143, "Join Up With Us," Be an Air-WAC
1944, 19½ × 28

Plate 144, Share the Deeds of Victory
1943, 28 × 42

Plate 145, Women Work for Victory
ca. 1942, 18 × 26

Plate 146, "The Girl of the Year Is a SPAR"
1942, 28 × 42

Plate 147, Be a Marine, Free a Marine
1942, 14 × 22

Plate 148, "Proud—I'll Say" Join the WAVES
1943, 28 × 42

Plate 149, Join Women's Land Army
1943, 20 × 28

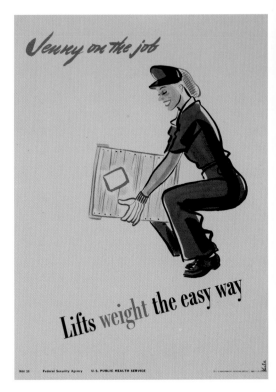

Plates 150-156, Jenny on the Job
1943, 10 × 14

Plate 157, I'll Carry Mine Too!
1943, 22 × 28

Plate 158, "Of Course I Can!"
1944, 18 × 25

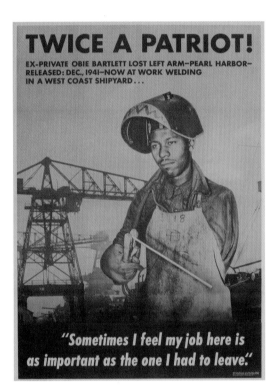

Plate 159, Twice a Patriot!
1943, 28 × 40

Plate 160, United We Win
1942, 28 × 40 *

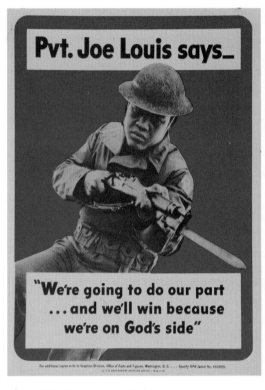

Plate 161, Pvt. Joe Louis Says_
1942, 17½ × 25 *

Plate 162, Build for the Future
1945, 18½ × 25

Plate 163, "Above and Beyond the Call of Duty"
1943, 20 × 28

Plate 164, Keep Us Flying! Buy War Bonds
1943, 22 × 28

Plate 165, Libres (the Four Freedoms)
ca. 1942, 20 × 28

Plate 166, Americanos Todos
1943, 22 × 26

WESTERN DEFENSE COMMAND AND FOURTH ARMY
WARTIME CIVIL CONTROL ADMINISTRATION
Presidio of San Francisco, California
April 24, 1942

INSTRUCTIONS
TO ALL PERSONS OF
JAPANESE
ANCESTRY
Living in the Following Area:

All of those portions of the Counties of Contra Costa and Alameda, State of California, within the boundary beginning at Carquinez Strait; thence southerly on U. S. Highway No. 40 to its intersection with California State Highway No. 4, at or near Hercules; thence easterly on said Highway No. 4 to its intersection with California State Highway No. 21; thence southerly on said Highway No. 21 to its intersection with California State Highway No. 24, at Walnut Creek; thence westerly on said Highway No. 24 to the southerly limits of the City of Berkeley; thence following the said southerly city limits to San Francisco Bay; thence northerly and following the shore line of San Francisco Bay, through San Pablo Strait, and San Pablo Bay, to the point of beginning.

Pursuant to the provisions of Civilian Exclusion Order No. 19, this Headquarters, dated April 24, 1942, all persons of Japanese ancestry, both alien and non-alien, will be evacuated from the above area by 12 o'clock noon, P. W. T., Friday, May 1, 1942.

No Japanese person living in the above area will be permitted to change residence after 12 o'clock noon, P. W. T., Friday, April 24, 1942, without obtaining special permission from the representative of the Commanding General, Northern California Sector, at the Civil Control Station located at:

2345 Channing Way, Berkeley, California.

Such permits will only be granted for the purpose of uniting members of a family, or in cases of grave emergency.

The Civil Control Station is equipped to assist the Japanese population affected by this evacuation in the following ways:

1. Give advice and instructions on the evacuation.

2. Provide services with respect to the management, leasing, sale, storage or other disposition of most kinds of property, such as real estate, business and professional equipment, household goods, boats, automobiles and livestock.

3. Provide temporary residence elsewhere for all Japanese in family groups.

4. Transport persons and a limited amount of clothing and equipment to their new residence.

The Following Instructions Must Be Observed:

1. A responsible member of each family, preferably the head of the family, or the person in whose name most of the property is held, and each individual living alone, will report to the Civil Control Station to receive further instructions. This must be done between 8:00 A. M. and 5:00 P. M. on Saturday, April 25, 1942, or between 8:00 A. M. and 5:00 P. M. on Sunday, April 26, 1942.

2. Evacuees must carry with them on departure for the Assembly Center, the following property:

(a) Bedding and linens (no mattress) for each member of the family;
(b) Toilet articles for each member of the family;
(c) Extra clothing for each member of the family;
(d) Sufficient knives, forks, spoons, plates, bowls and cups for each member of the family;
(e) Essential personal effects for each member of the family.

All items carried will be securely packaged, tied and plainly marked with the name of the owner and numbered in accordance with instructions obtained at the Civil Control Station.

The size and number of packages is limited to that which can be carried by the individual or family group.

3. No pets of any kind will be permitted.

4. The United States Government through its agencies will provide for the storage at the sole risk of the owner of the more substantial household items, such as iceboxes, washing machines, pianos and other heavy furniture. Cooking utensils and other small items will be accepted for storage if crated, packed and plainly marked with the name and address of the owner. Only one name and address will be used by a given family.

5. Each family, and individual living alone, will be furnished transportation to the Assembly Center or will be authorized to travel by private automobile in a supervised group. All instructions pertaining to the movement will be obtained at the Civil Control Station.

Go to the Civil Control Station between the hours of 8:00 A. M. and 5:00 P. M., Saturday, April 25, 1942, or between the hours of 8:00 A. M. and 5:00 P. M., Sunday, April 26, 1942, to receive further instructions.

J. L. DeWITT
Lieutenant General, U. S. Army
Commanding

SEE CIVILIAN EXCLUSION ORDER NO. 19.

Plate 167, To All Persons of Japanese Ancestry
1942, 8½ × 14

"No loyal citizen of the United States should be denied the democratic right to exercise the responsibilities of his citizenship, regardless of his ancestry.

"The principle on which this country was founded and by which it has always been governed is that Americanism is a matter of the mind and heart.

"Americanism is not, and never was, a matter of race or ancestry.

"Every loyal American citizen should be given the opportunity to serve this country wherever his skills will make the greatest contribution—whether it be in the ranks of our armed forces, war production, agriculture, government service, or other work essential to the war effort."

THE PRESIDENT OF THE UNITED STATES, FEBRUARY 3, 1943

OWI Poster No. 75. Additional copies may be obtained upon request from the Division of Public Inquiries, Office of War Information, Washington, D. C.

Plate 168, "Americanism Is not a Matter of Race"
1943, 20 × 28

Plate 169, Plant a Victory Garden
1942, 22 × 28

Plate 170, Your Victory Garden
1945, 19 × 26½

Plate 171, Can All You Can
1943, 16 × 22½

Plate 172, U.S. Needs Us Strong
ca. 1942, 13 × 20

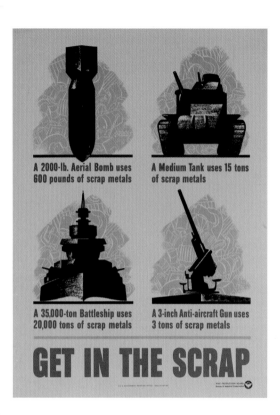

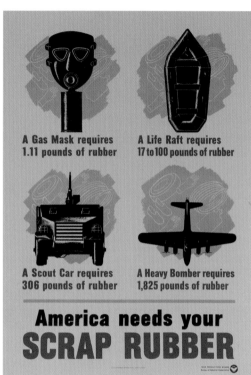

Plates 173-175, American Scrap Drives
1942, 22 × 28

Plate 176, Save Waste Fats
1943, 20 × 28 *

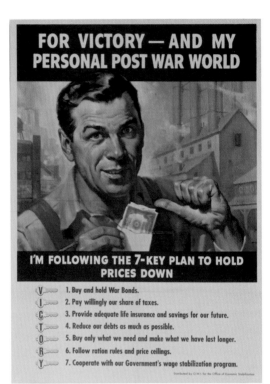

Plates 177-179, The 7 Key Plan
1942, 20 × 28

Plate 180, Defense Needs Rubber
1941, 28 × 40

Plate 181, Today Every Fire Helps Hitler
1942, 12 × 16

Plate 182, Strike Down This Monster!
1942, 14 × 18

Plate 183, Our Carelessness
1943, 22 × 28

careless matches aid the Axis

PREVENT FOREST FIRES !

Plate 184, Careless Matches Aid the Axis
1942, 18 × 24 *

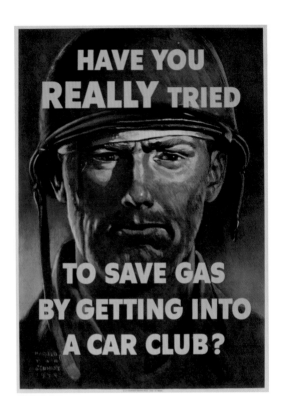

Plate 185, Have You Really Tried
1944, 28 × 40

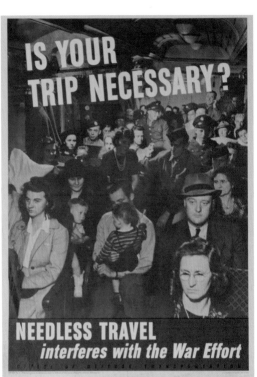

Plate 186, Is Your Trip Necessary?
1943, 20 × 28

Plate 187, Me Travel? ...Not This Summer
1945, 26 × 37 *

Plate 188, When You Ride Alone
1943, 20 × 28

Plate 189, Clear the Tracks for War Shipments
ca. 1942, 28 × 20

Plate 190, Don't Shiver Next Winter
1944, 18½ × 26

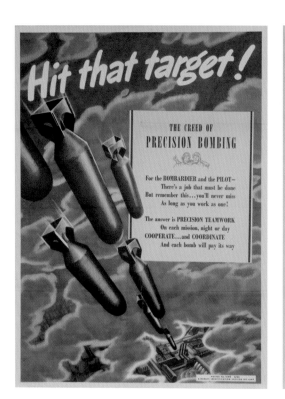

Plates 191-194, Precision Bombing
1942, 18 × 25

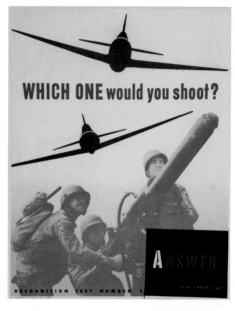

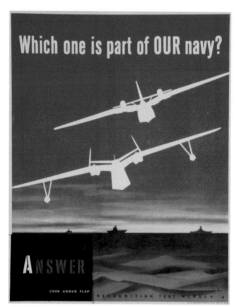

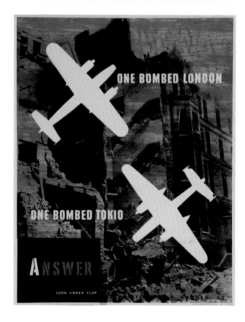

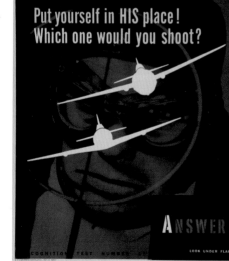

Plates 195-204, Recognition Tests
1943, 11 × 14

★ 141 ★

RULES of the ROAD

Running LIGHTS

AVA DEPT. U.S.N.T.S. SAMPSON, N.Y.

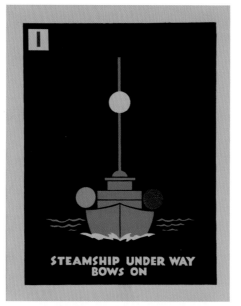

1

STEAMSHIP UNDER WAY
BOWS ON

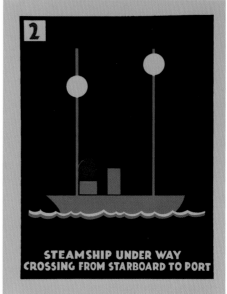

2

STEAMSHIP UNDER WAY
CROSSING FROM STARBOARD TO PORT

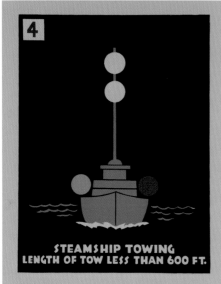

4

STEAMSHIP TOWING
LENGTH OF TOW LESS THAN 600 FT.

5

STEAMSHIP TOWING TWO SHIPS
LENGTH OF TOW OVER 600 FT.

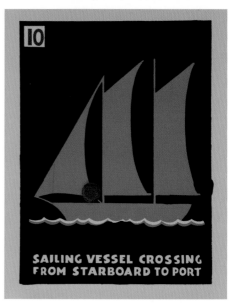

10

SAILING VESSEL CROSSING
FROM STARBOARD TO PORT

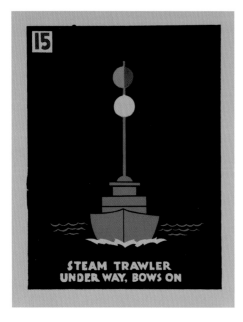

15

STEAM TRAWLER
UNDER WAY, BOWS ON

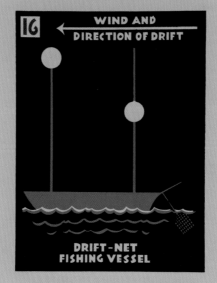

16

WIND AND
DIRECTION OF DRIFT

DRIFT-NET
FISHING VESSEL

22

ROWBOATS
UNDER OARS

Plates 205-214, Rules of the Road
ca. 1943, 11½ × 14

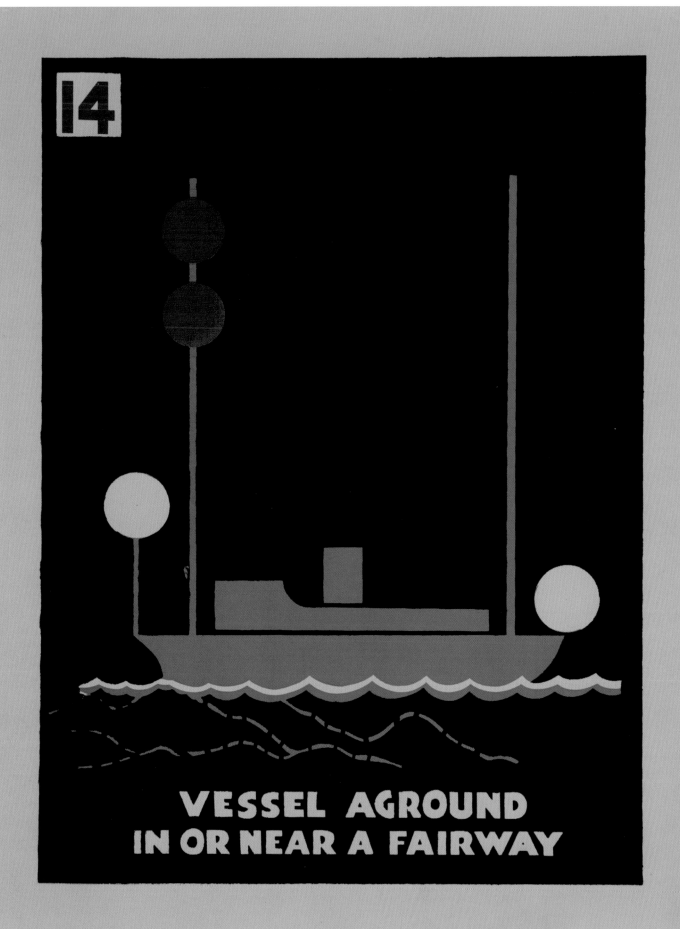

VESSEL AGROUND
IN OR NEAR A FAIRWAY

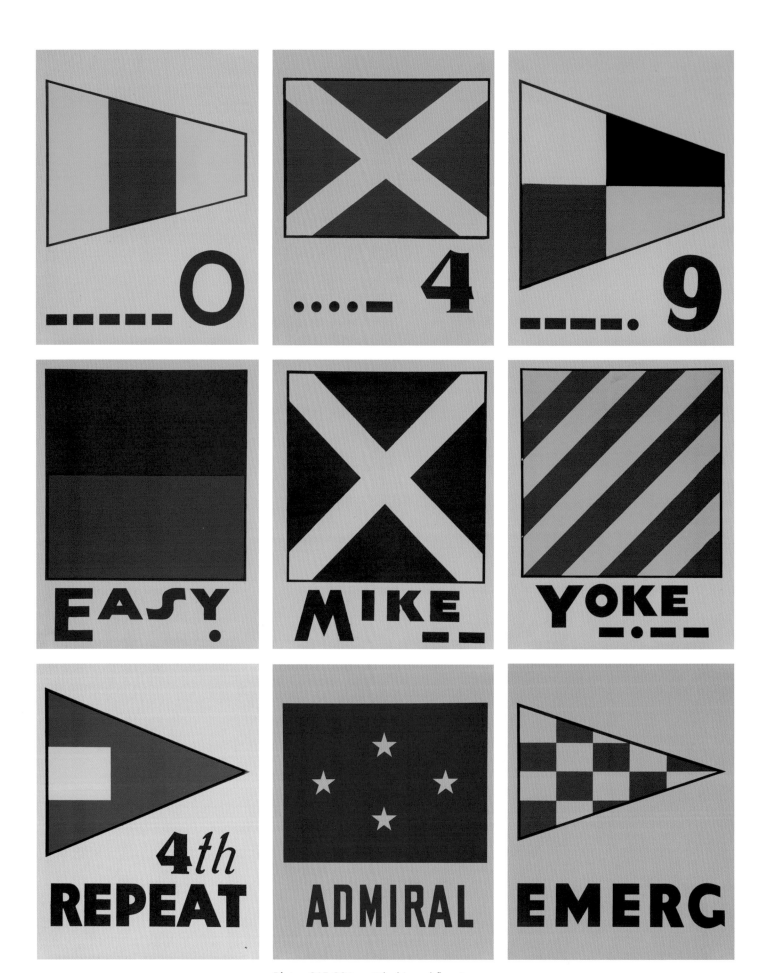

Plates 215-224, untitled (naval flags)
ca. 1943, 11½ × 14

COMMISSION
PENNANT

Plates 225-227, Loose Talk Can Cost Lives
1942, 14 × 22

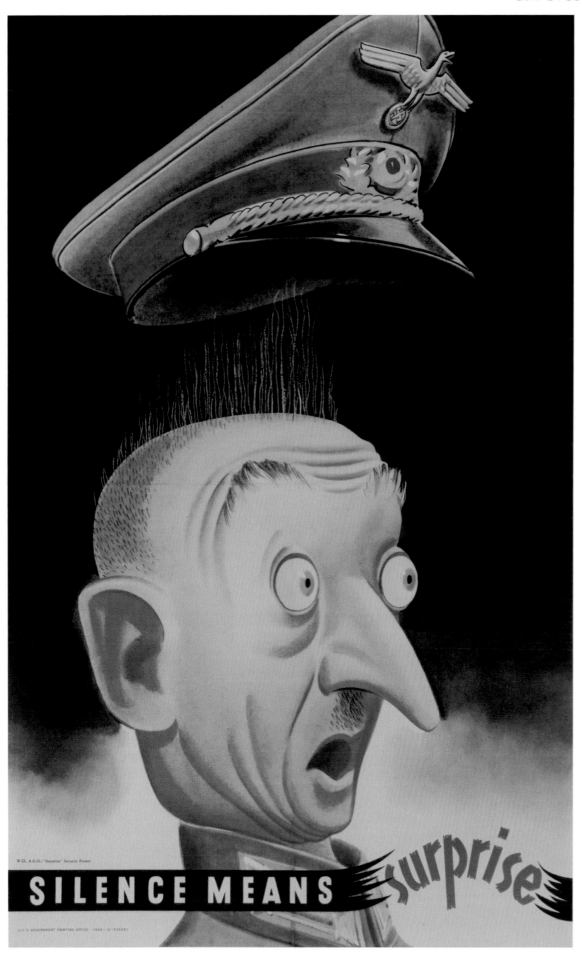

Plate 228, Silence Means Surprise
1943, 14½ × 22½

Plate 229, ... Because Somebody Talked!
1944, 20 × 28 *

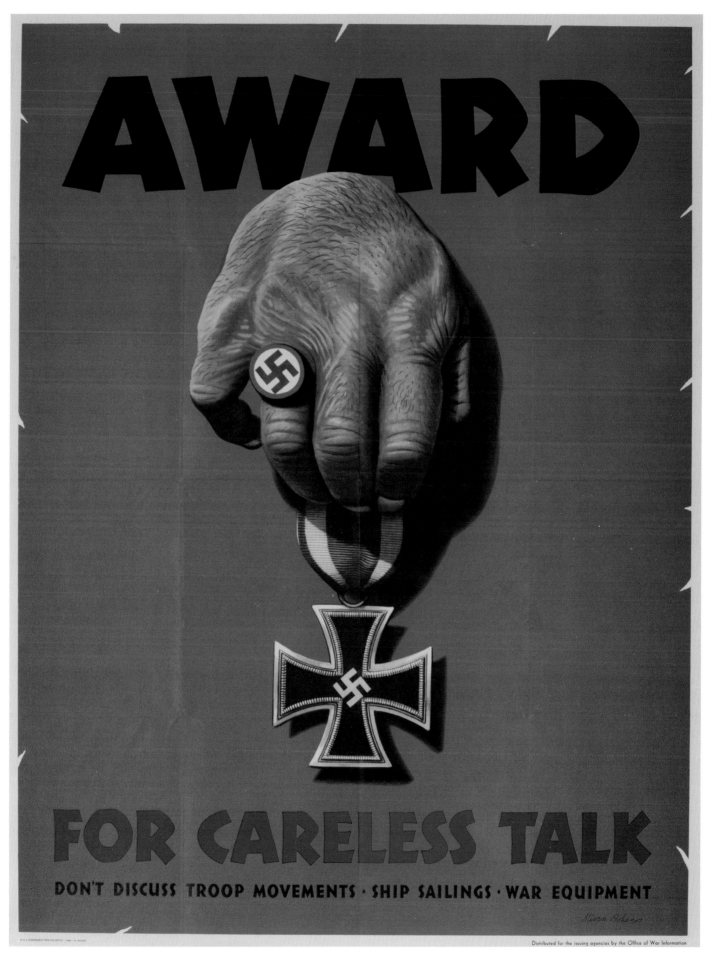

Plate 230, Award for Careless Talk
1944, 20 × 28 *

Plate 231, Wanted! For Murder
1944, 28 × 40 *

Plate 232, Someone Talked!
1944, 28 × 40

Plate 233, Bits of Careless Talk
1943, 20 × 28 *

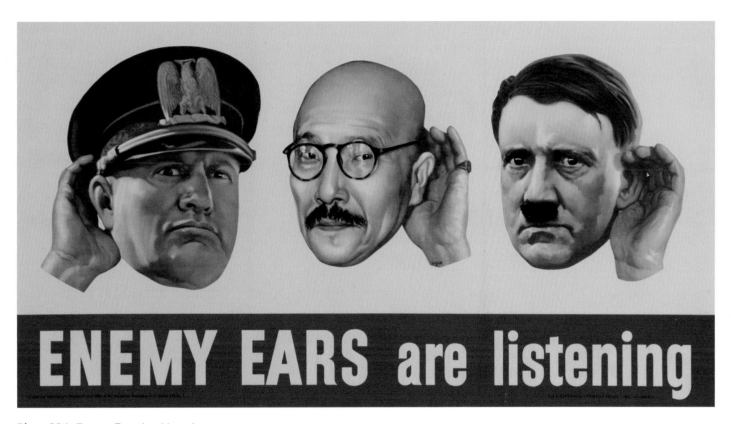

Plate 234, Enemy Ears Are Listening
1942, 26 × 13½

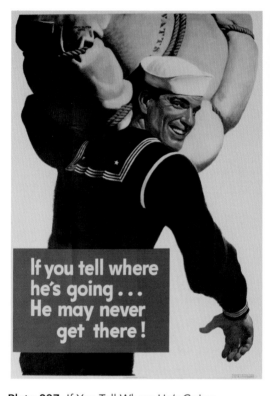

Plate 235, Careless Talk ... Got There First
1944, 28 × 40 *

Plate 236, I'm Counting on You!
1943, 28 × 40 *

Plate 237, If You Tell Where He's Going...
1943, 28 × 40

Plate 238, Less Dangerous Than Careless Talk
1944, 28 × 40

Plate 239, If You Tell Where They're Going
1943, 28 × 40

Plate 240, A Careless Word... A Needless Loss
1943, 22 × 28 *

Plate 241, We Caught Hell!
1944, 28 × 40

Plate 242, He's Watching You
1944, 28 × 40 *

Plate 243, Give 'Em Both Barrels
1941, 40 × 30 *

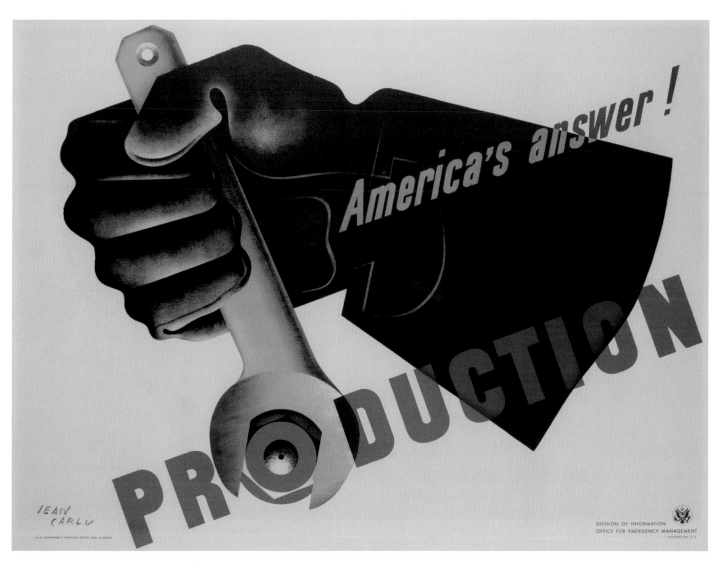

Plate 244, America's Answer! Production
1942, 40 × 30

Plate 245, Don't Let Him Down!
1941, 30 × 40

Plate 246, Give It Your Best!
1942, 40 × 28 *

Plates 247-248, Keep 'Em Rolling!
1941, 30 × 40

KEEP 'EM ROLLING!

DIVISION OF INFORMATION
OFFICE FOR EMERGENCY MANAGEMENT
WASHINGTON, D.C.

Plate 249, Next Stop Tokyo—Let's Go!
1945, 28 × 42

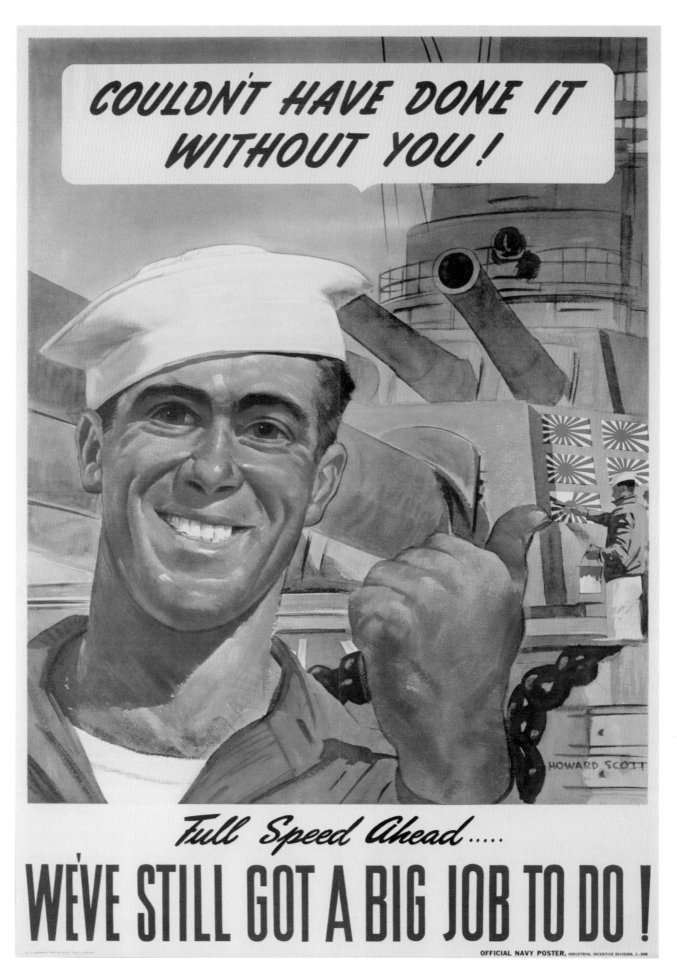

Plate 250, We've Still Got a Big Job to Do!
1943, 28 × 42

Plate 251, Pour it On!
1942, 28½ × 40½*

Plate 252, Let's Give Him Enough and on Time
1942, 40½ × 28½

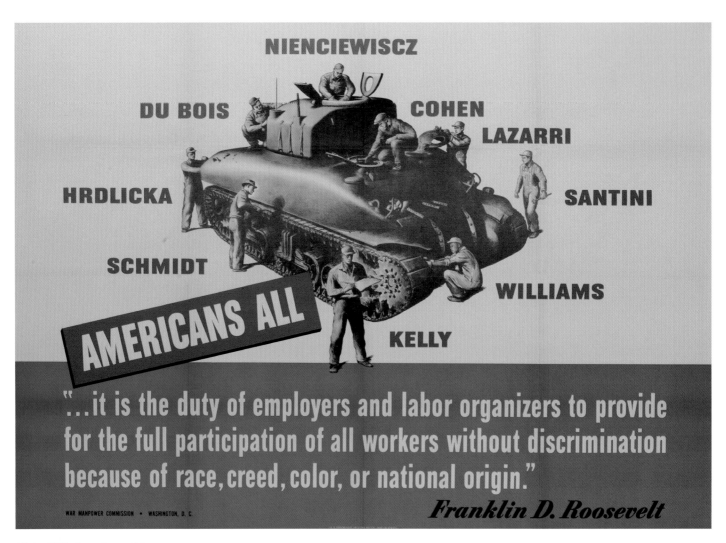

Plate 253, Americans All
1942, 40 × 28

Plate 254, You Help Build the B-29
1945, 36 × 26

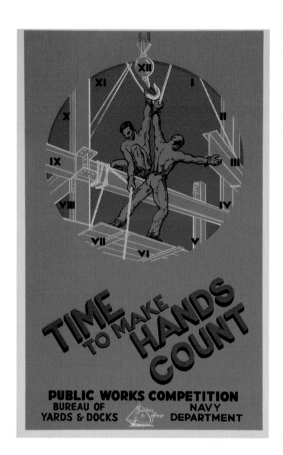

Plates 255 -258, Bureau of Yards and Docks
ca. 1942, 14 × 22

CONSERVE CONSTRUCTION EQUIPMENT

BY PROPER MAINTENANCE & REPAIR

BURY THE AXIS

BUREAU OF YARDS & DOCKS — NAVY PUBLIC WORKS AWARDS — NAVY DEPARTMENT

Plate 259, You Knock 'Em Out, More Production
1942, 28 × 42

Plate 260, Kinda Give It Your Personal Attention
ca. 1944, 28 × 40

MILES OF HELL
to Tokyo!

WORK WHERE YOU'RE NEEDED

CONSULT YOUR U.S. EMPLOYMENT SERVICE OFFICE

WAR MANPOWER COMMISSION

Plate 261, Miles of Hell to Tokyo!
1945, 18 × 26

Plate 262, God Help Me If This Is a Dud!
1942, 28 × 42

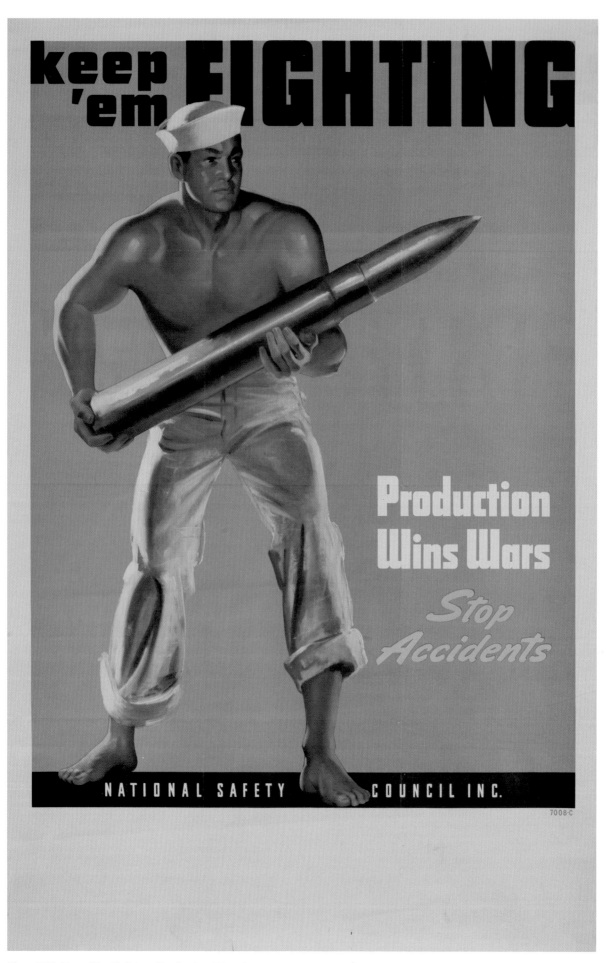

Plate 263, Keep 'Em Fighting, Production Wins Wars
ca. 1942, 25 × 37

Plate 264, I'm Proud of You Folks Too!
1944, 40 × 28

Plate 265, Get the Jap and Get it Over!
1945, 20 × 28

Plate 266, Work to Win or You'll Work For Him
ca. 1943, 15 × 20

Plate 267, Produce for Your Navy
ca. 1943, 28 × 42

Plate 268, They'll Let Us Know When to Quit!
1944, 20 × 28

Plate 269, Our Fighters Deserve Our Best
1942, 28 × 40

Plate 270, Bundles for Berlin, More Production!
1942, 28 × 40

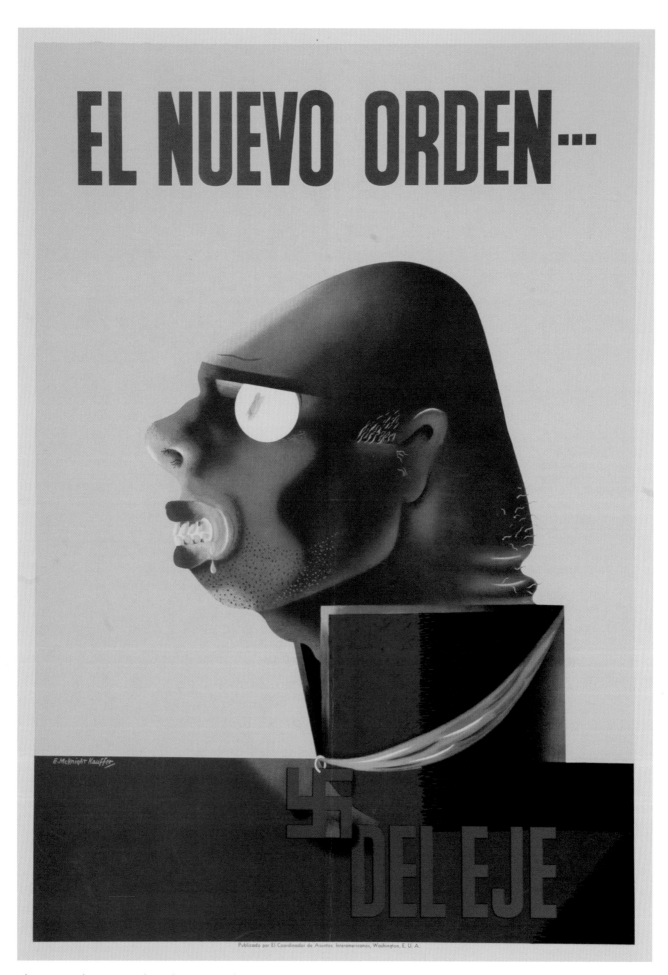

Plate 271, El Nuevo Orden (The New Order)
ca. 1943, 14½ × 20

...*we here highly resolve that these dead shall not have died in vain*...

REMEMBER DEC. 7th!

Plate 272, Remember Dec. 7th!
1942, 28 × 40 *

Plate 273, We French Workers Warn You...
1942, 40 × 28

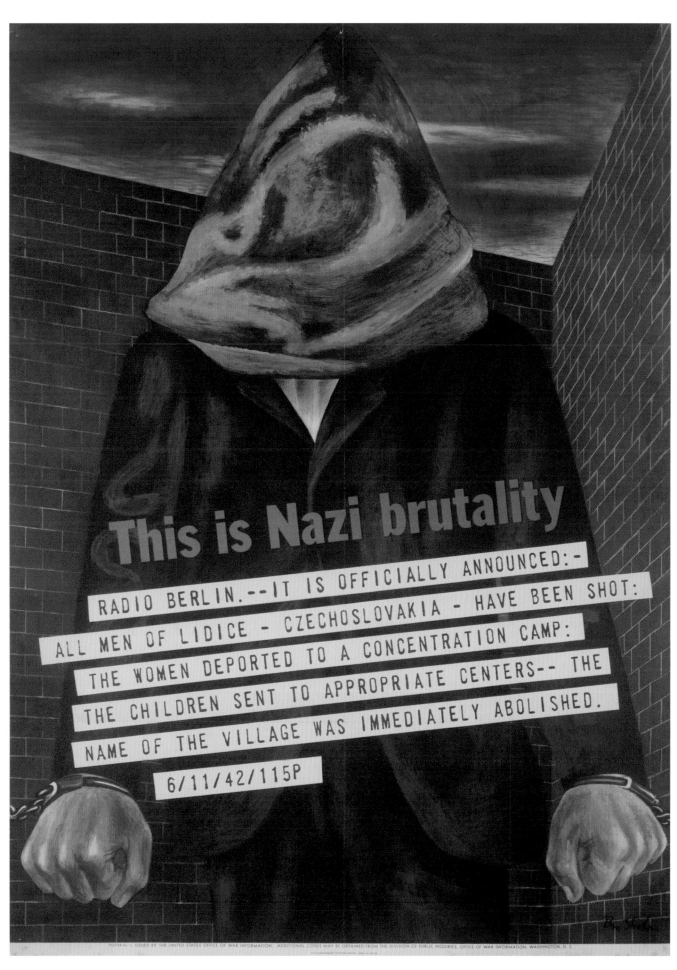

Plate 274, This Is Nazi Brutality
1942, 28 × 40

Plate 275, Avenge December 7
1942, 28 × 40 *

Plate 276, Americans Will Always Fight
1943, 28 × 40 *

Plate 277, What Do You Say, America?
1942, 7 × 10 *

Plate 278, The Nazis Burned These Books
1943, 20 × 28

Plate 279, What Do You Say, America?
1942, 7 × 10 *

LIBERTY LIVES ON
450TH ANNIVERSARY OF THE DISCOVERY OF AMERICA, 1492-1942

Plate 280, Liberty Lives On
1942, 26 × 40

Plate 281, Help Britain Defend America
ca. 1941, 18 × 28

Plate 282, Speed Up America
ca. 1940, 25 × 45

Plate 283, Lest We Regret ... Defend America
ca. 1940, 18 × 28

Plate 284, Britain Must Win
ca. 1941, 17 × 25

Plate 285, China... Looks to Us!
ca. 1945, 14 × 22

Plate 286, China Shall Have Our Help!
ca. 1944, 14 × 22 *

Plates 287-288, United Nations Fight for Freedom
1942, 20 × 28 *

THE UNITED NATIONS FIGHT FOR FREEDOM

UNITED STATES | GREAT BRITAIN | SOVIET RUSSIA | CHINA
AUSTRALIA | BELGIUM | BRAZIL | CANADA
COSTA RICA | CUBA | CZECHOSLOVAKIA | DOMINICAN REPUBLIC
EL SALVADOR | ETHIOPIA | GREECE | GUATEMALA
HAITI | HONDURAS | INDIA | LUXEMBOURG
MEXICO | NETHERLANDS | NEW ZEALAND | NICARAGUA
NORWAY | PANAMA
PHILIPPINES | POLAND
SOUTH AFRICA | YUGOSLAVIA

Plate 289, Help British War Victims
ca. 1942, 14 × 22

Plate 290, Help Now!
ca. 1942, 17 × 24

Plate 291, "Thumbs Up"
ca. 1942, 14 × 22

Plate 292, British War Relief Society
ca. 1942, 15 × 21

Plate 293, Keep Faith with Them
1942, 12 × 17

Plate 294, Many Campaigns in One
ca. 1942, 21 × 28

Plate 295, Now Is the Time... Give!
ca. 1942, 13 × 20

Plate 296, Don't Say "No" to the U.S.O.
ca. 1942, 21 × 11

Plate 297, Join American Red Cross
1942, 30 × 20

Plate 298, War Relief, Give! American Red Cross
ca. 1941, 13 × 20

Plate 299, Their Fight Is Our Fight
ca. 1946, 14 × 22

Plate 300, untitled (Chain Him)
1941, 28 × 20

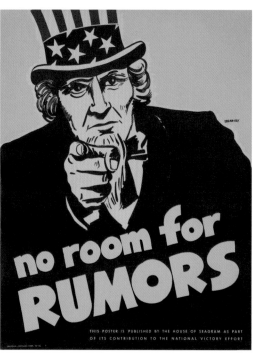

Plates 301-304, House of Seagram
ca. 1942, 21 × 28

Plates 305-306, House of Seagram
ca. 1942, 21 × 28

EVEN IN THIS
FRIENDLY TAVERN
THERE MAY BE
ENEMY EARS

STOP LOOSE TALK · RUMORS

THIS POSTER IS PUBLISHED BY THE HOUSE OF SEAGRAM AS PART
OF ITS CONTRIBUTION TO THE NATIONAL VICTORY EFFORT

SEAGRAM—DISTILLERS CORP., N.Y.C. 4

Plates 307-310, Calvert Distillers Corp.
ca. 1942, 17 × 25

One Year's Liquor Industry Taxes could Buy 1,236 Bombers

Remember PROHIBITION?
Don't let it happen again!

CONTRIBUTED AS A PUBLIC SERVICE BY CALVERT DISTILLERS CORP., N.Y.C.   SERIES 2-E

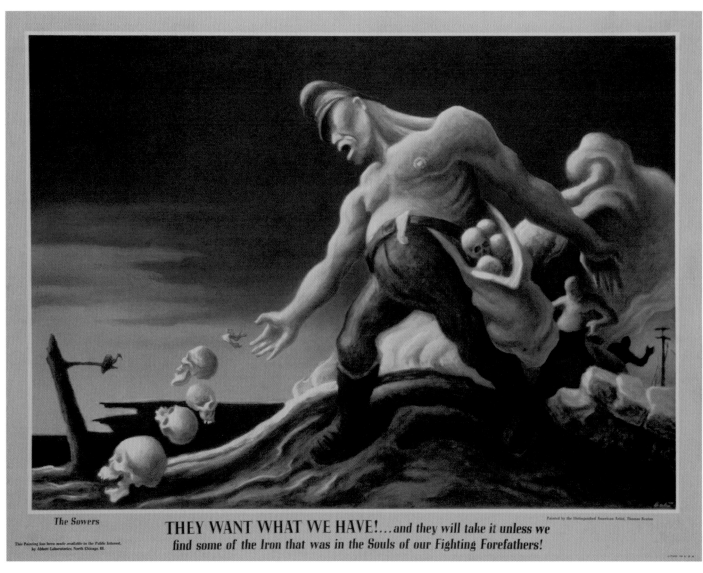

The Sowers

THEY WANT WHAT WE HAVE!...and they will take it unless we
find some of the Iron that was in the Souls of our Fighting Forefathers!

Plate 311, The Sowers, Abbott Laboratories
1942, 23½ × 18 *

Plate 312, Again, Abbott Laboratories
1942, 23½ × 20¾ *

PRIDE OF THE FLEET

Plates 313-314, EBCo, Electric Boat Company
1943, 24 × 19

SINKING JAP SHIP FROM OFFICIAL U.S NAVY PHOTO TAKEN THROUGH PERISCOPE

COPYRIGHT 1943, ELECTRIC BOAT COMPANY, NEW YORK

REVENGE IN THE PACIFIC

Plates 315-318, This Is America for This We Fight
ca. 1943, 20 × 30

THIS IS AMERICA
—*for this we fight*

Mt. Rushmore National Memorial, Honoring Washington, Jefferson, Theodore Roosevelt and Lincoln

Heroes of the Republic—
An Inspiration to the Heroes of Today

Plate 319, What Matters Most, Penn. Railroad
ca. 1942, 25 × 42

YOU can help

SAVE TELEPHONE SERVICE FOR WAR NEEDS

Don't call INFORMATION for numbers in the directory

MARCH - 1942

Plate 320, You Can Help, Save Telephone Service
1942, 25 × 38

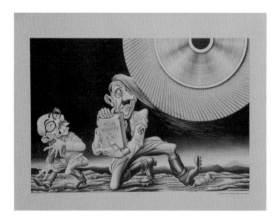

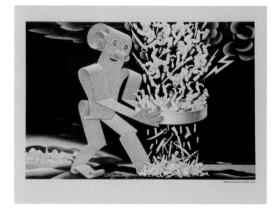
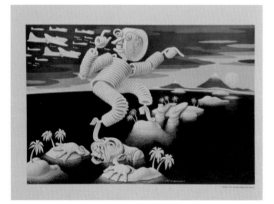

Plates 321-330, untitled (Wickwire Steel)
1942-1944, 21 × 17

Let's Bury the Tramps—with Bonds and Stamps!

Three Blind Rats!

Let's Hit 'em Hard, America!

"Look Out, Boys . . . They're Loaded!"

Put Your Money in the SOCK !

"You Said It, Boys!"

Plates 331-337, Philco Radio
1941-1944, 18 × 12

Keep 'Em Frying!

Plate 338, It's Great to Be Helping Uncle Sam
ca. 1944, 9 × 12

Plate 339, "Victory Through Airpower"
1943, 16 × 17

Plates 340-341, The New Haven Rail Road
ca. 1943, 28 × 42

RIGHT OF WAY
for Fighting Might!

Countless trainloads of fighting men and materials are thundering through southern New England every hour of the night and day... in a grim symphony of determination to win this war at all costs!

A giant task force of over 27,000 New Haven Railroaders are working around the clock... meeting the constant pressure for more and more trains, longer trains, heavier loads, faster freight schedules... and at the same time, are chalking up new records of efficiency in railroad operation and maintenance.

War now comes first in everybody's timetable! Troops and fighting tools, essential raw materials, food, gasoline, coal and fuel oil must get through. If this should result in occasional inconvenience or delay in getting you to your destination, we know you will understand that we are doing our best to serve you and the Nation!

HERE'S HOW YOU CAN HELP!

1. Always consult latest timetable before making a trip. Train schedules are subject to sudden changes during wartime.

2. Purchase rail and Pullman tickets well in advance of departure... and cancel promptly if plans change.

3. Avoid peak travel periods. Travel MID-week if possible.

4. Travel light and check all baggage not needed on train.

5. Be considerate of your fellow passenger, sharing the coach seat... and making sure your baggage is placed securely in rack.

6. Be patient if you have to wait for a seat in the Diner. Relinquish your seat promptly. Reason: we have 75% more mouths to feed these days.

7. Keep mum about the war... with people you meet on the train.

THE *NEW HAVEN* R.R.

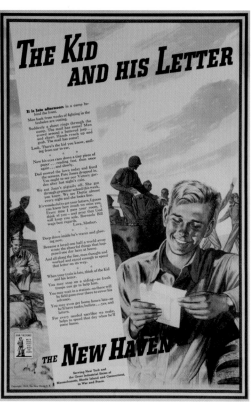

Plates 342-345, The Kid, New Haven Rail Road
ca. 1943, 28 × 42

Plate 346, Buy More War Bonds and Stamps
1942, 24 × 36

Plate 347, This Is the Enemy
1942, 24 × 36

Plates 348-349, Consolidated Edison System
ca. 1943, 13½ × 18

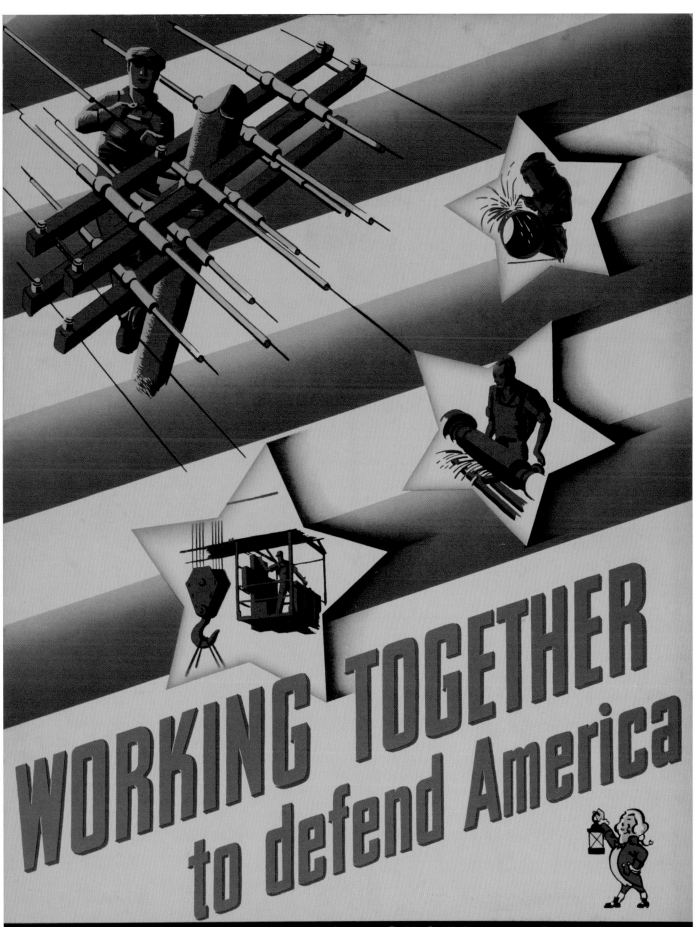

WORKING TOGETHER
to defend America

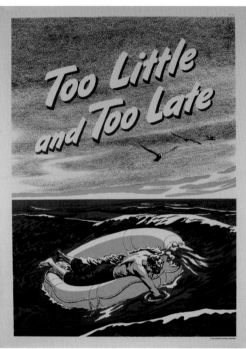

Plates 350-352, General Electric Company
1942, 38 × 50½ *

Plate 353, Step On It!
1942, 30 × 40

Plates 354-355, Oldsmobile Division
1942, 30 × 40

Plate 356, In the Army ... Behind the Army
ca. 1942, 30 × 40

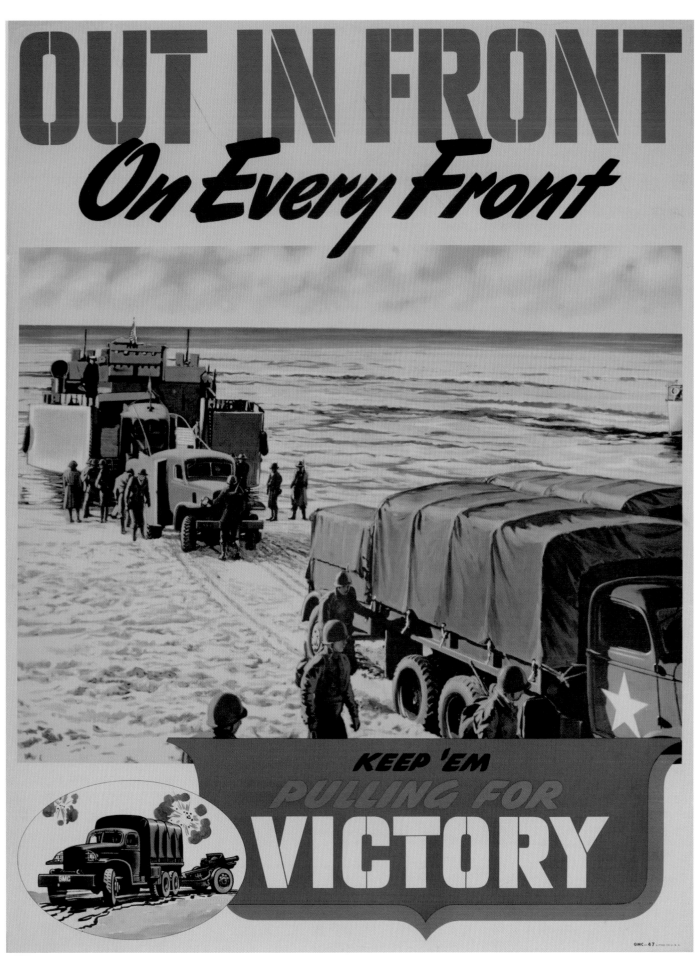

Plate 357, Out in Front, On Every Front
ca. 1942, 30 × 40

Plates 358-359, The Saturday Evening Post
1941-1942, 22 × 28

Plate 360, Keep it Under Your Stetson
ca. 1942, 30 × 40

Plate 361, The Pack to Take—Kools
ca. 1942, 20 × 30

Plate 362, Cette Fois Jusqu'à Berlin
ca. 1944, 40 × 30

Plate 363, untitled (Allies breaking swastika)
1944, 26 × 19

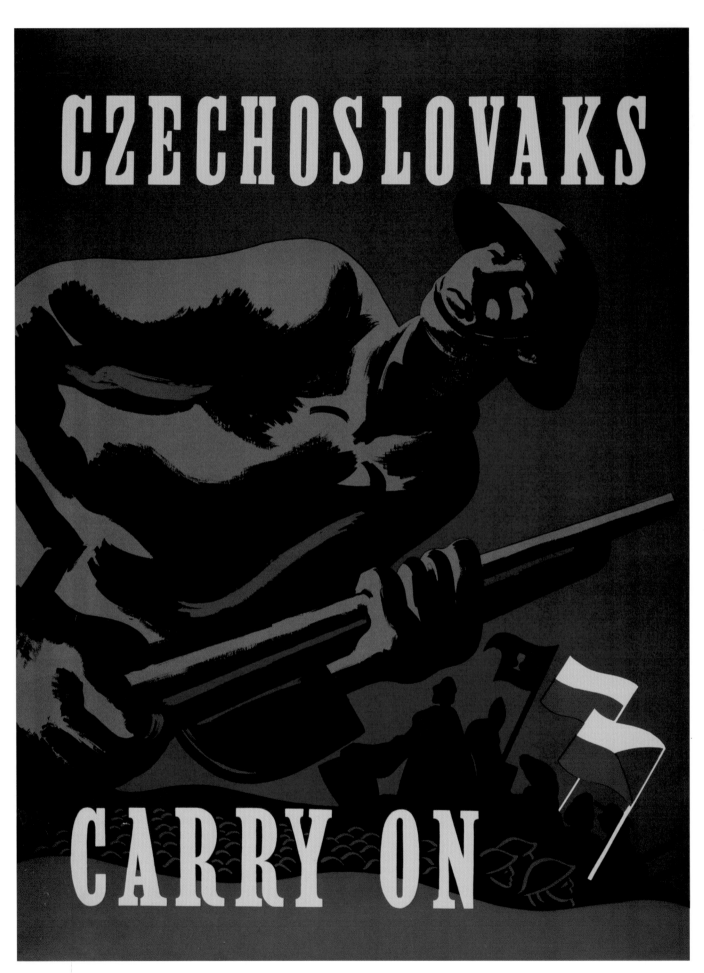

Plate 364, Czechoslovaks Carry On
1942, 24 × 32

Plate 365, New Zealand Fights
1942, 24 × 32

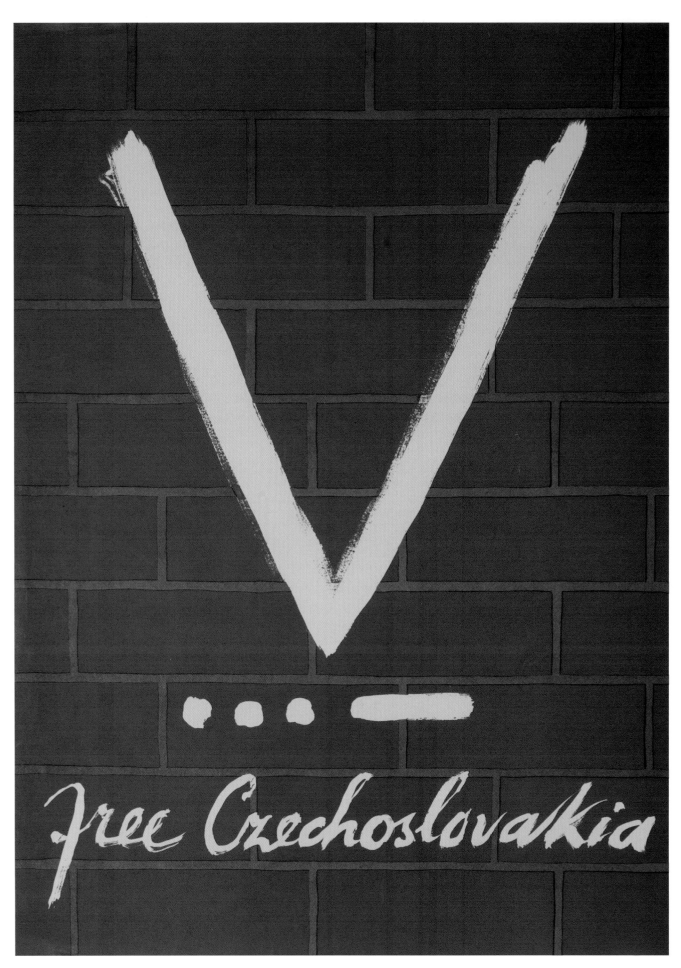

Plate 366, V Free Czechoslovakia
ca. 1943, 17½ × 24

Plate 367, Wanted in Prague
ca. 1943, 17½ × 24

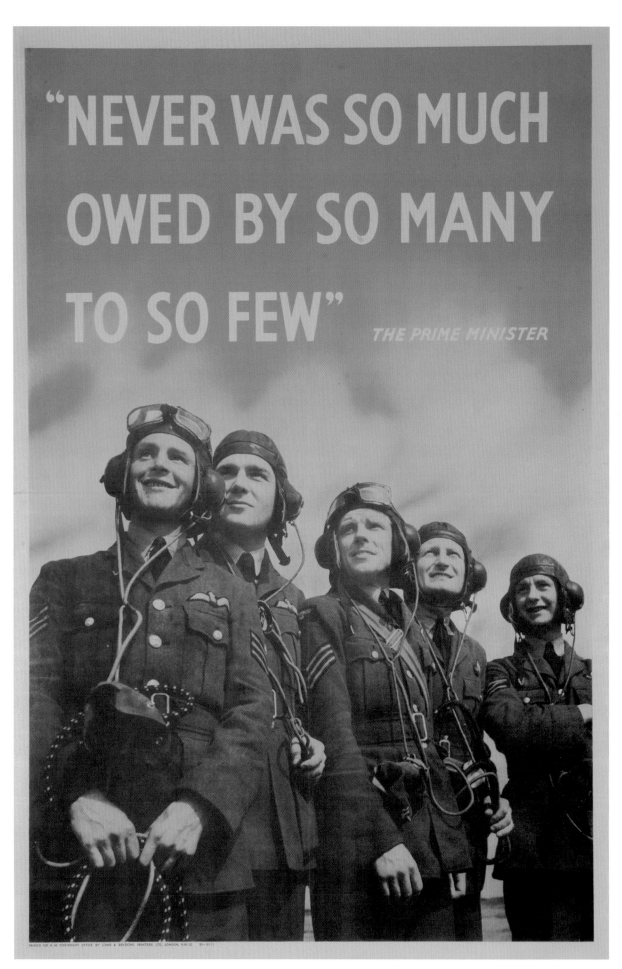

Plate 368, "Never Was so Much Owed"
ca. 1940, 20 × 30

Plate 369, "Let Us Go Forward Together"
ca. 1940, 20 × 30

Plate 370, You Are Wanted Too!
ca. 1940, 19 × 30

Plate 371, Join the WRENS
ca. 1940, 20 × 30 *

Plate 372, Serve in the WAAF
ca. 1940, 20 × 30

Plate 373, Take the Road to Victory, Join the WAAF
ca. 1940, 20 × 30

Plate 374, Leaders of the Royal Air Force
1941, 30 × 20

Plate 375, The Royal Navy
1939, 15 × 20

Plate 376, She's in the Ranks Too!
ca. 1940, 20 × 30

A MESSAGE FROM

HER MAJESTY THE QUEEN

TO THE NURSES OF BRITAIN

My thoughts go out to the women who, in this third year of War, are serving the cause of humanity in every branch of the Nursing Profession.

May you be granted strength and courage to carry on your selfless labours and may you find your reward in the gratitude of those to whom you minister.

Elizabeth R

Plate 377, A Message from Her Majesty
ca. 1943, 10 × 15

Plate 378, Scrap It
1942, 20 × 30

Plate 379, Six Health Hints
ca. 1942, 20 × 30

Plate 380, Splinters Are Poisoned Arrows
1942, 20 × 30

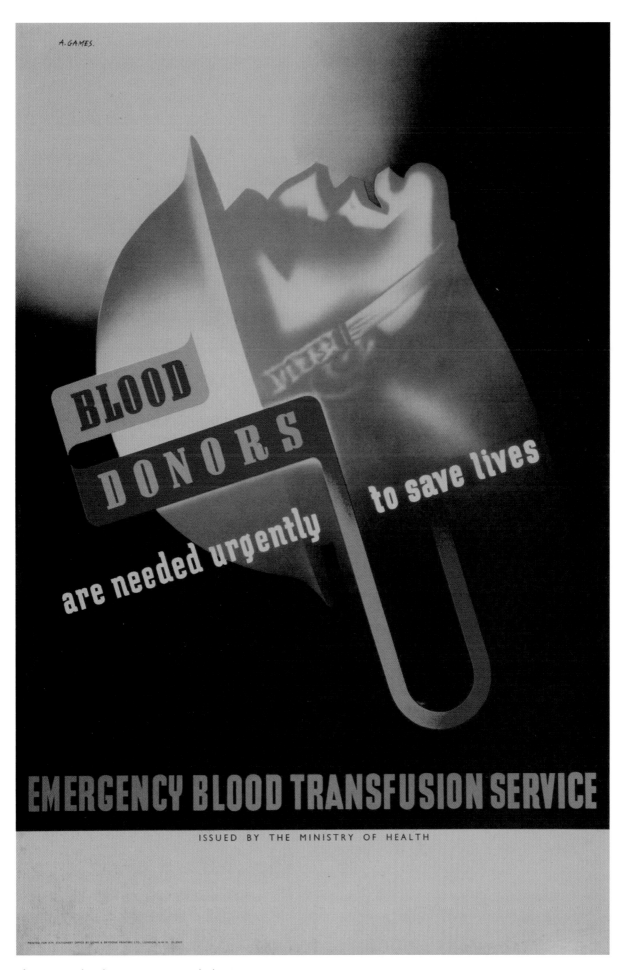

Plate 381, Blood Donors Are Needed
ca. 1942, 13 × 19

Plate 382, Save for Defence
ca. 1942, 20 × 30

Plate 383, More Ships—Come On!
ca. 1942, 10 × 15

Plate 384, The Signal Is Save
ca. 1942, 10 × 15

Plate 385, Save for Victory
ca. 1942, 20 × 30

Plate 386, Join the Crusade Buy Defence Bonds
ca. 1942, 20 × 30 *

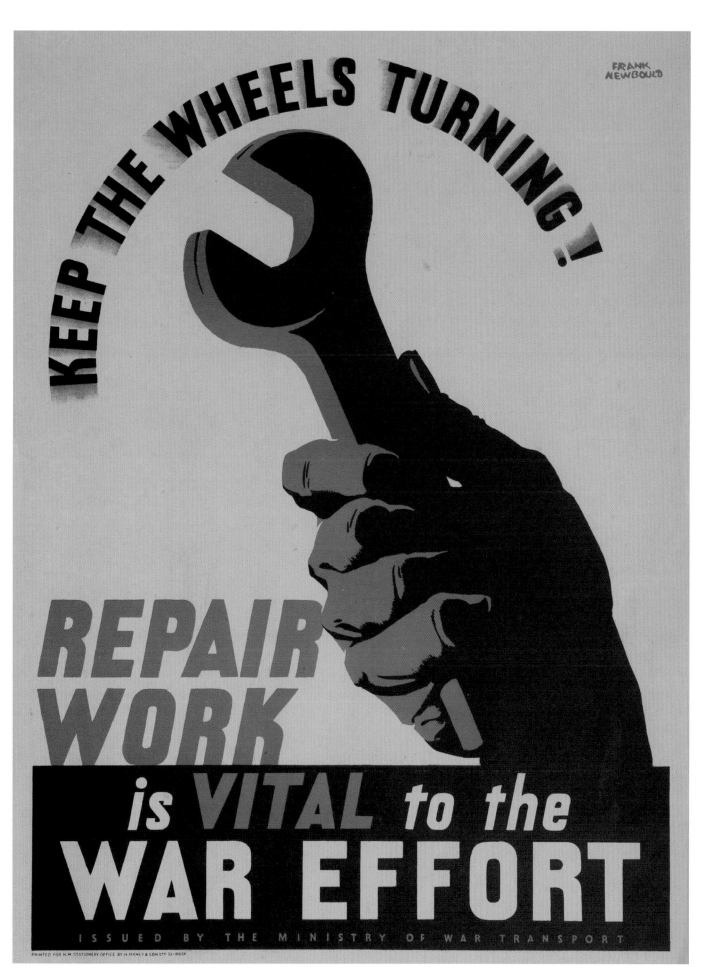

KEEP THE WHEELS TURNING!

FRANK NEWBOULD

REPAIR WORK is VITAL to the WAR EFFORT

ISSUED BY THE MINISTRY OF WAR TRANSPORT

PRINTED FOR H.M. STATIONERY OFFICE BY H.MANLEY & SON LTD 51-8658

Plate 387, Keep the Wheels Turning
ca. 1942, 15 × 20

Plate 388, Keep Mum—She's Not so Dumb!
ca. 1942, 20 × 30

Plate 389, Keep Mum She's Not so Dumb!
1942, 10 × 15 *

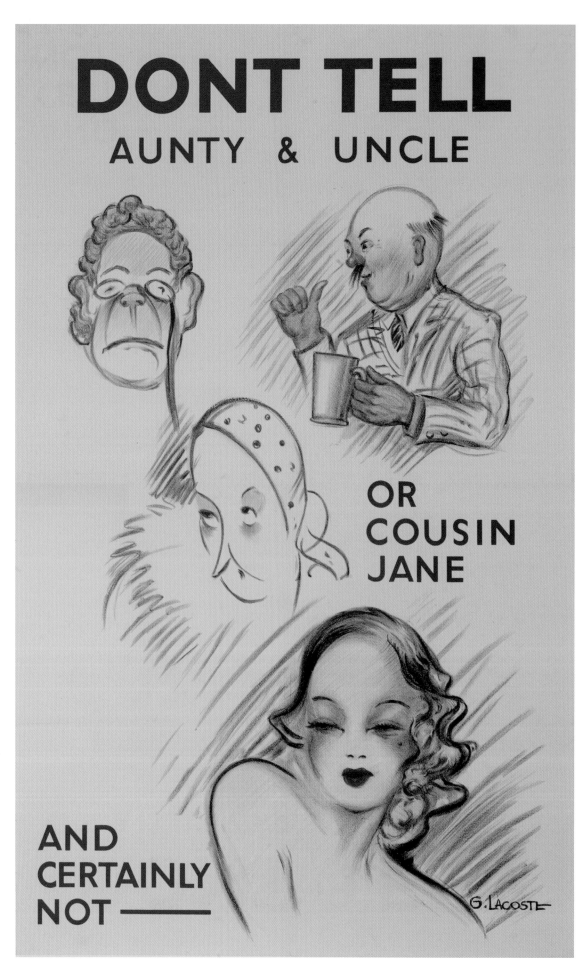

Plate 390, Don't Tell Aunty & Uncle
ca. 1942, 25 × 39½

A FEW
CARELESS WORDS
MAY END IN THIS—

Many lives were lost in the last war through careless talk
Be on your guard ! Don't discuss movements of ships or troops

Printed for H.M. Stationery Office by Greycaine Ltd., Watford and London. T 51- 8667

Plate 391, A Few Careless Words
ca. 1942, 15 × 20 *

Plates 392-395, Careless Talk Costs Lives
1943, 8 × 12½

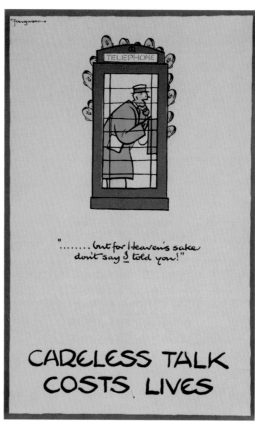

Plates 396-399, Careless Talk Costs Lives
1943, 8 × 12½

Plate 400, For Bombs Like These
ca. 1942, 20 × 30 *

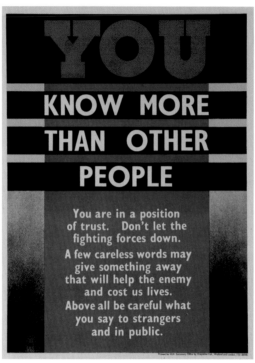

Plate 401, You Know More Than Other People
ca. 1942, 20 × 30 *

Plate 402, We're Waiting to Start
ca. 1942, 20 × 30 *

PORTS ARE OFTEN BOMBED WHEN CONVOYS ARE IN BECAUSE SOMEBODY TALKED

Never mention arrivals, sailings, cargoes or destinations to anybody.

Printed for H.M. STATIONERY OFFICE BY GILBT WHITEHEAD & CO., LTD. NEW ELTHAM, S.E.9 51-2024

Plate 403, Ports Are Often Bombed
ca. 1942, 13½ × 20

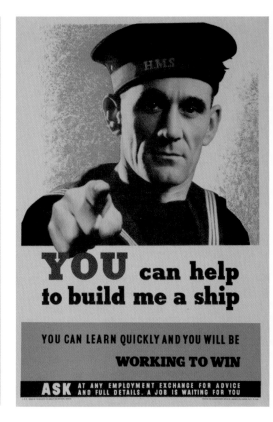

Plates 404-406, You Can Help to Build
ca. 1942, 20 × 30 *

Plate 407, If You Can't Go to the Factory
ca. 1942, 19 × 28½

Plate 408, Great Britain Will Pursue the War
ca. 1945, 20 × 30

PER ARDVA AD ASTRA

NEVER IN THE
FIELD OF HUMAN
CONFLICT, HAVE
SO MANY OWED
SO MUCH TO SO
FEW. WINSTON CHURCHILL

Plate 409, Never in the Field of Human Conflict
ca. 1940, 17 × 22

A British "Commando" raid on a German-held port in Norway

BACK THEM UP!

La captura del submarino alemán U 570 por un "Hudson" Lockheed de la Jefatura Costera Británica.

¡LA GRAN BRETAÑA DEFENSORA DE LA LIBERTAD!

The bombing in daylight of the power station at Knapsack, Germany, by the Royal Air Force.

BACK THEM UP!

British field-guns smash a German tank attack at point-blank range in Libya

BACK THEM UP!

A British cruiser ramming an Italian submarine in the Mediterranean

BACK THEM UP!

A British tank attack in the Western Desert

BACK THEM UP!

Plates 410-416, Back Them Up!
ca. 1942, 20 × 30

"Hurricanes" of the Royal Air Force co-operating with the Russian Air Force.

BACK THEM UP!

PRINTED IN ENGLAND by CHROMOWORKS LTD LONDON. 51-2326.

Plate 417, Together
ca. 1942, 20 × 30

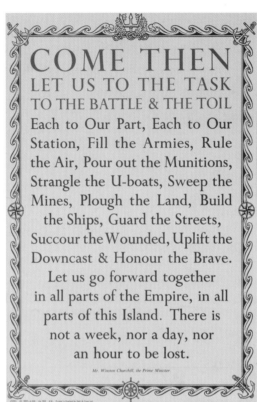

Plate 418, Come Then Let Us to the Task
ca. 1941, 10 × 15

Plate 419, One by One, His Legs Will Be Broken
ca. 1942, 20 × 30

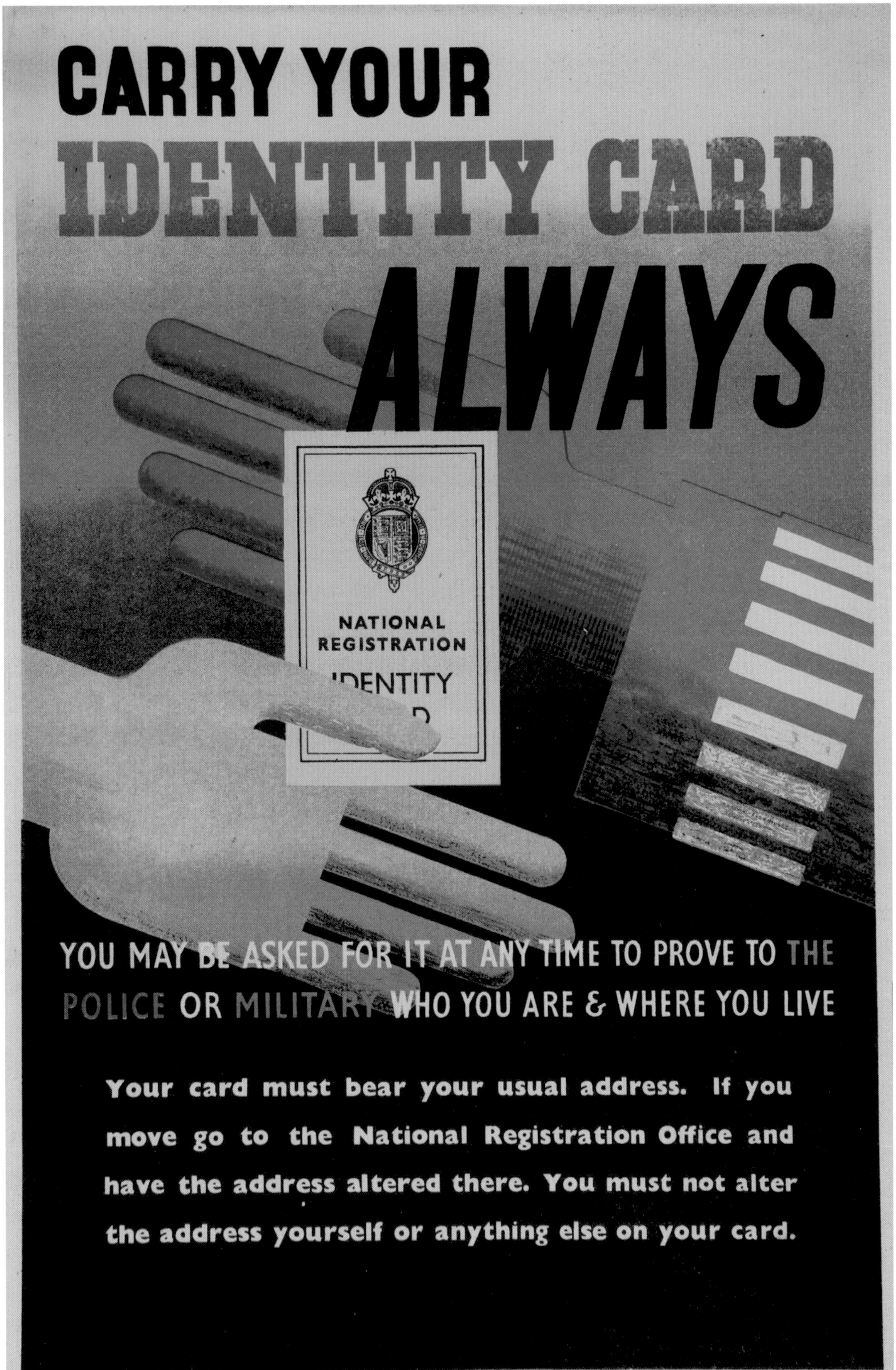

Plate 420, Carry Your Identity Card
ca. 1942, 10 × 15

Plate 421, Buses Give Way to Tanks
ca. 1942, 20 × 30

Plate 422, Travel Between Times
ca. 1942, 20 × 30

Plate 423, The Life-line Is Firm
ca. 1942, 20 × 30

Plate 424, Children Are Safer in the Country
ca. 1942, 10 × 15

Plate 425, Mightier Yet! Britain's Mechanised Army
ca. 1942, 20 × 30

Plate 426, King George's Fund for Sailors
1947, 20 × 30

Plate 427, untitled (Tanks)
ca. 1944, 20 × 30

Plate 428, untitled (Airfield)
ca. 1944, 20 × 30

Plate 429, The Torch; Be Yours to Hold It High!
ca. 1942, 12 × 18 *

Plate 430, Canada's New Army
ca. 1941, 24 × 36

Plate 431, All Aboard! Buy Victory Bonds
ca. 1943, 36 × 24

Plate 432, You Serve by Saving
ca. 1942, 19 × 26

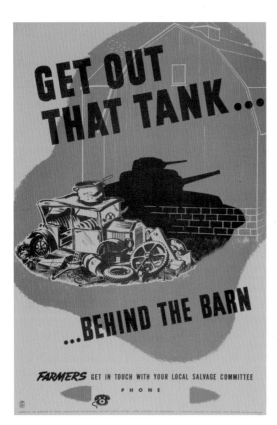

Plate 433, Get Out That Tank...
ca. 1942, 12 × 18

Plate 434, It's Got to Fit ...
ca. 1942, 24 × 36

Plate 435, Roll Out the Rubber
ca. 1942, 12 × 18

Plate 436, We're in the Army Now
ca. 1942, 10 × 15

Plates 437-443, National Salvage Office
ca. 1942, 10 × 15 *

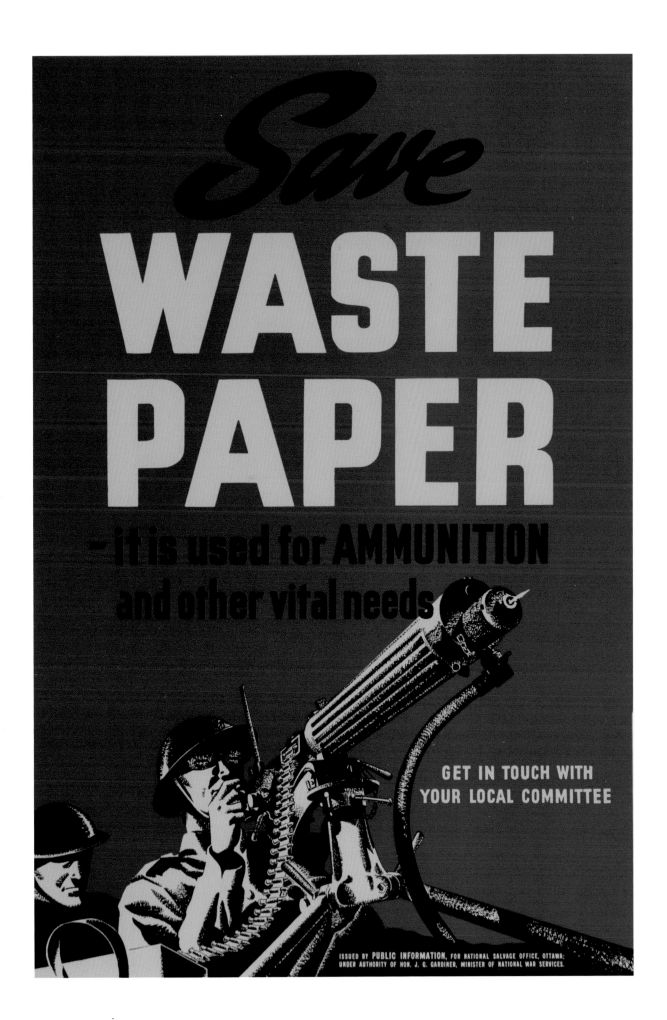

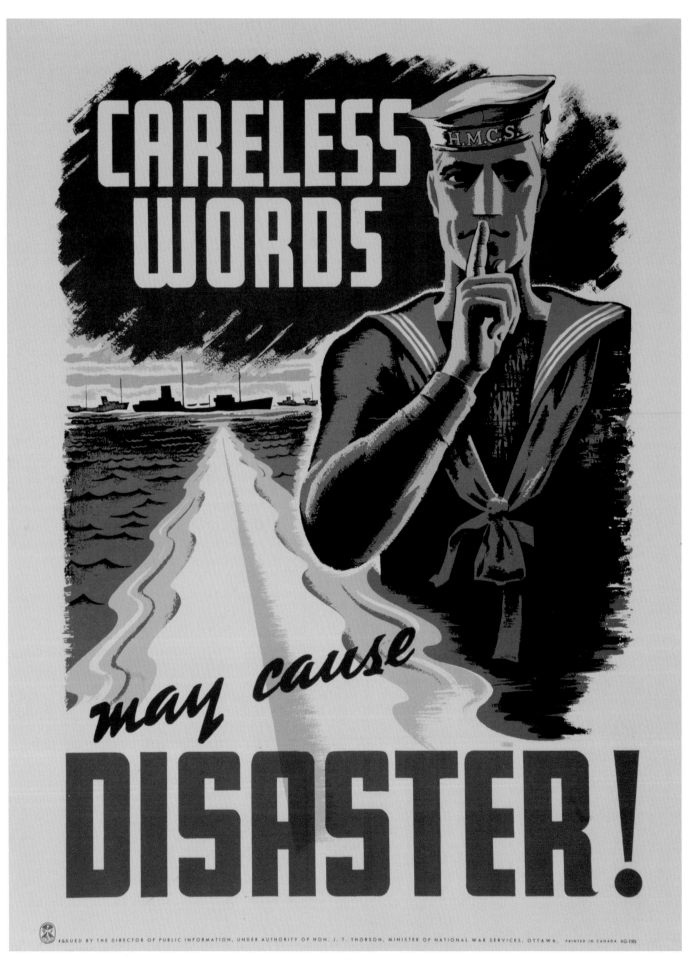

Plate 444, Careless Words May Cause Disaster!
ca. 1942, 9 × 12

Plate 445, The Walls Have Ears
ca. 1942, 18 × 24

Plate 446, A Workman Gossiped
ca. 1942, 13½ × 20

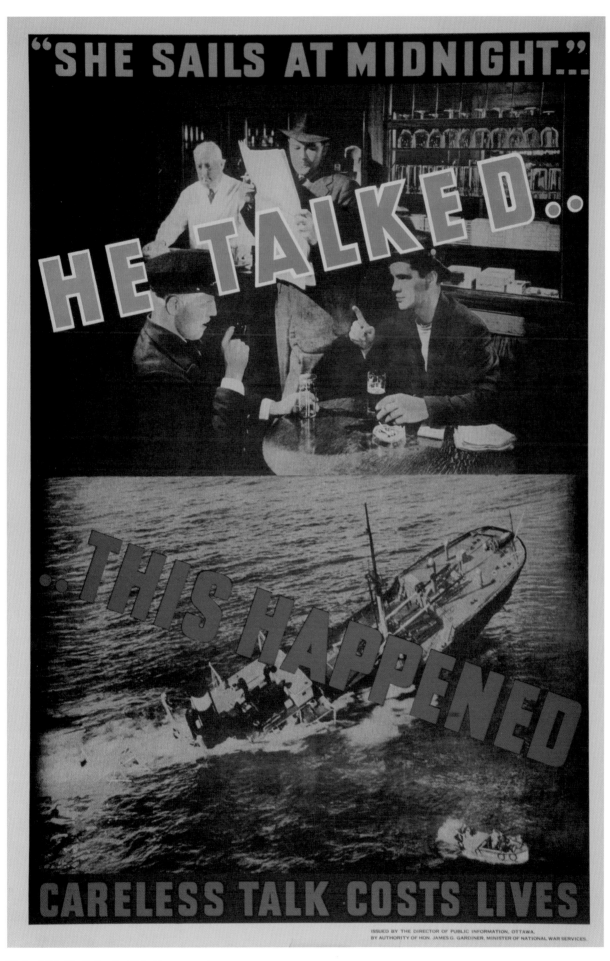

Plate 447, He Talked....This Happened
ca. 1942, 13½ × 20

Plate 448, Shoptalk May Be Sabotalk
ca. 1944, 18 × 24½

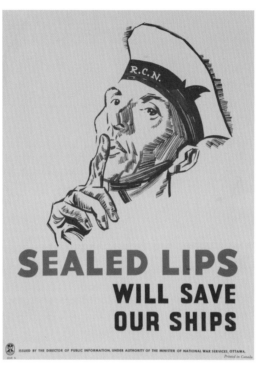

Plate 449, Sealed Lips Will Save Our Ships
ca. 1942, 9 × 12

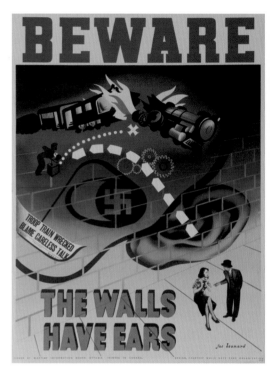

Plate 450, Beware the Walls Have Ears
ca. 1942, 18 × 24½

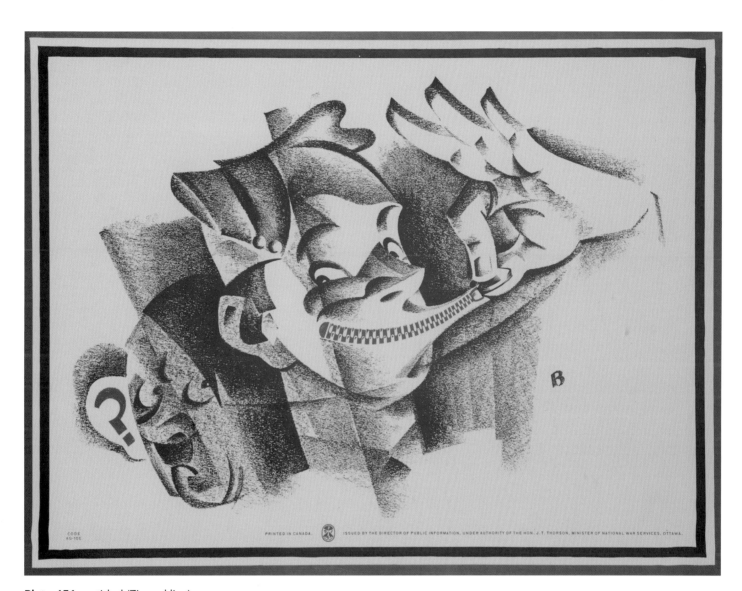

Plate 451, untitled (Zipped lips)
ca. 1942, 16½ × 12½

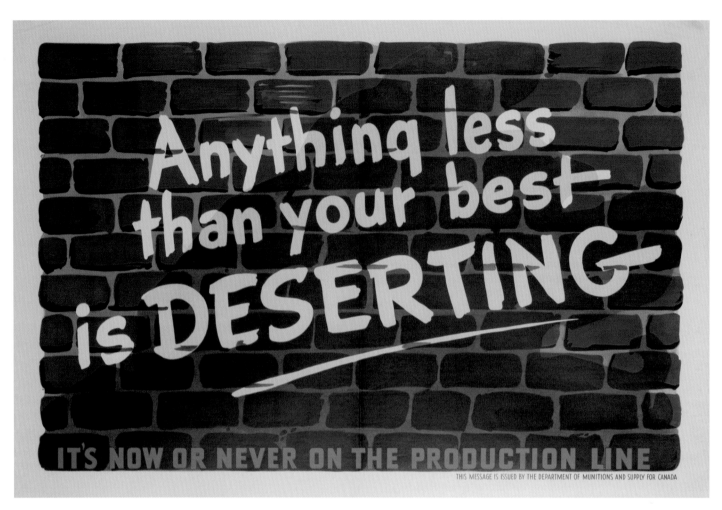

Plate 452, Anything Less than Your Best is Deserting
ca. 1942, 36 × 24

Plate 453, The Lives of These Men
ca. 1942, 20 × 30

Plate 454, My Needle Hums Along
ca. 1942, 18 × 24

Plate 455, If You Don't Need It... Don't Buy it
ca. 1942, 18 × 24½

Plate 456, Thousands Are Waiting
ca. 1942, 18 × 24

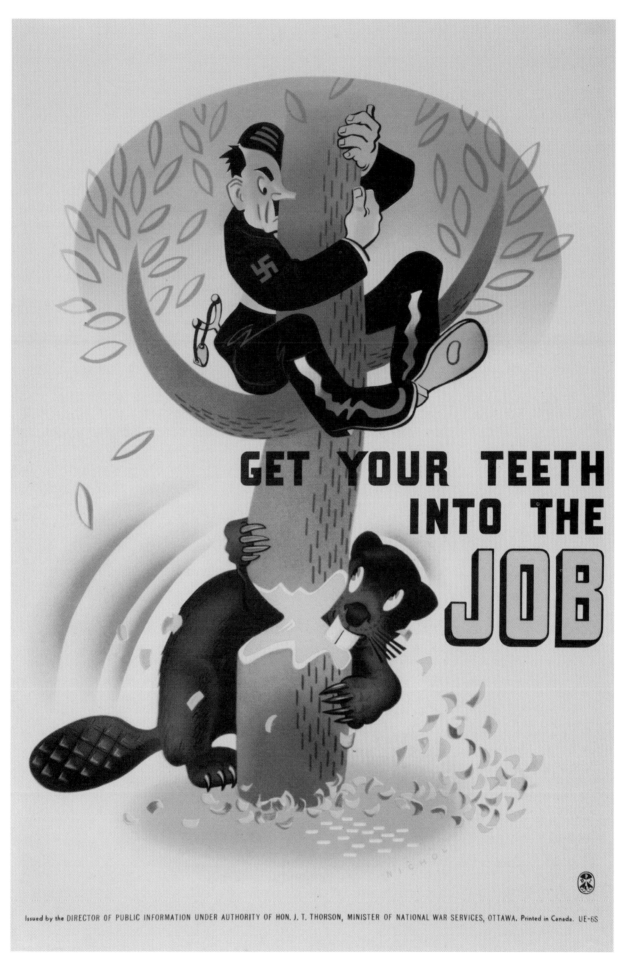

Plate 457, Get Your Teeth into the Job
ca. 1942, 9 × 13½

Plate 458, Nous Luttons Aussi!
ca. 1942, 20 × 30

POUR LA LIBERTÉ

TOUS LES HOMMES – TOUS LES OUTILS

Notre drapeau a toujours été le symbole de nos libertés: pensée, parole, justice, religion, droit d'association. Pour gagner cette guerre dont dépendent ces libertés, nos marins, nos soldats, nos aviateurs doivent avoir les armes nécessaires — plus d'armes et de meilleures armes que nos ennemis.

DES NAVIRES · DES CHARS D'ASSAUT · DES AVIONS · DES CANONS

Les techniciens et l'outillage de l'industrie canadienne de la pâte et du papier contribuent à accélérer la production de ces armes pour nos braves qui sont sous les drapeaux, en fabriquant des pièces pour les engins de guerre.

Ouvriers — nous avons une tâche à remplir — *accomplissons-la de tout coeur!* Travaillons soigneusement — travaillons avec précision — *travaillons allégrement!*

WARTIME MACHINE SHOP BOARD · CANADIAN PULP & PAPER ASSOCIATION

Wartime Machine Shop Board · Canadian Pulp & Paper Association apporte cette contribution à l'effort de guerre du Canada sans aucune rémunération.

Plate 459, Pour la Liberté
ca. 1942, 20 × 30

Plate 460, It's Our War
ca. 1942, 21 × 31

Plate 461, Every Canadian Must Fight
ca. 1942, 12 × 17

Plate 462, Whatever Your Job May Be Fight
ca. 1942, 21 × 31

Plate 463, To Victory
ca. 1942, 9 × 13½

Plate 464, Lick Them over There!
ca. 1942, 12 × 18 *

Plate 465, Let's Go ... Canada!
ca. 1942, 12 × 18

Plate 466, Teamwork, Thanks Pal!
ca. 1942, 21 × 31

Plate 467, Lets Go! Step It Up Boys!
ca. 1942, 21 × 39

Plate 468, Keep Them Both Flying!
ca. 1942, 20 × 30

Plate 469, To Protect Our Freedom
ca. 1942, 21½ × 33

Plate 470, Roll 'em Out!
ca. 1942, 21 × 31

Plate 471, This Means D-E-L-A-Y
ca. 1942, 39 × 31

Plate 472, Wanted Magazines for Our Fighting Men
ca. 1942, 10 × 15

Plate 473, Send the Boys Good Books
ca. 1942, 12 × 18

Plate 474, Hold Your Tongue
ca. 1942, 8½ × 12½

Plate 475, War on Waste
ca. 1942, 13½ × 19½

Plate 476, Stick to Your Dancing, Soldier!
1942, 24 × 26

Plate 477, When You Leave Work Forget It!
ca. 1942, 22 × 30½

Plates 478-480, Australian 4th Liberty Loan
1943, 19½ × 29½

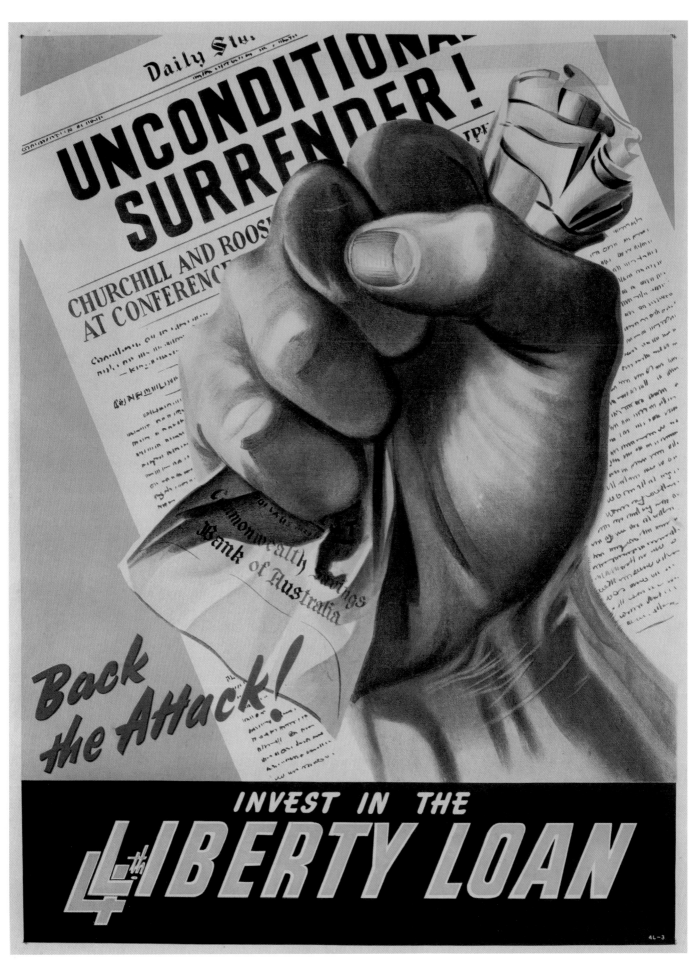

Plate 481, Back the Attack! 4th Liberty Loan
1943, 29½ × 39½

Plate 482, New Zealand Fights in Pacific Skies
ca. 1942, 32½ × 24½

Plate 483, New Zealand Fights for the Future
ca. 1941, 28 × 22

Plate 484, Liberation
1944, 30 × 45½

Plate 485, Libération
1944, 30 × 45½

Plate 486, 1934-XII Si
1934, 26 × 37

Plate 487, Nur Hitler (Only Hitler)
1932, 20 × 28½

Plate 488, Yudan Taiteki (Take Care of Fire)
ca. 1942, 12 × 28

Plate 489, Rules for Air Defense
ca. 1943, 22 × 32

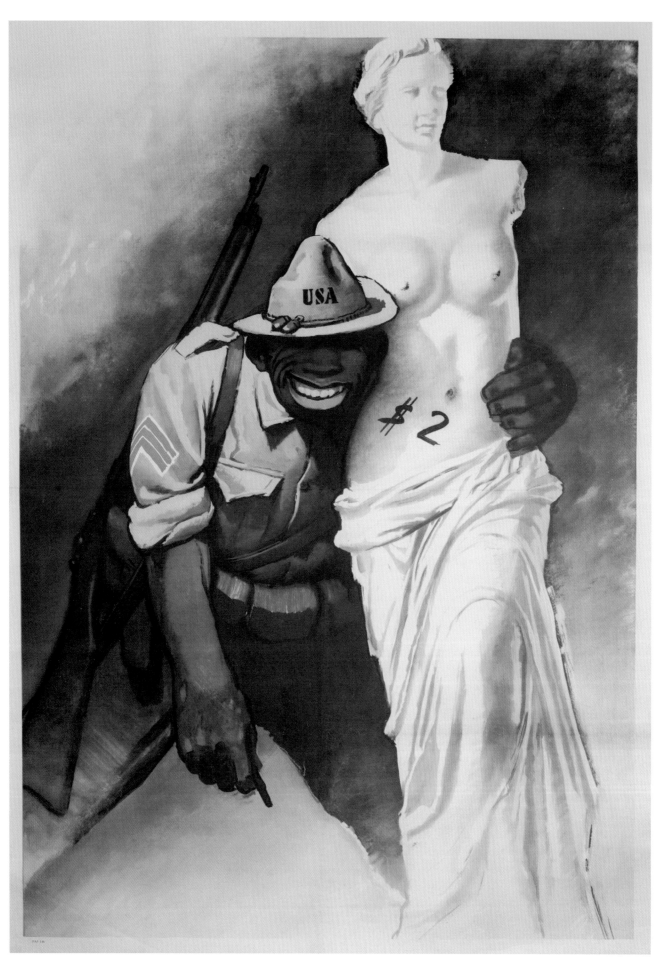

Plate 490, untitled ($2 Venus de Milo)
ca. 1942, 37 × 50

Plate 491, untitled (Soldier plundering church)
ca. 1942, 28 × 40

Plate 492, Confiance... (Confidence)
ca. 1942, 31 × 46

Plate 493, Achtüng Spione (Beware Spies)
ca. 1943, 22½ × 33

Plates 494-497, European Recovery Program
1950, 21½ × 29

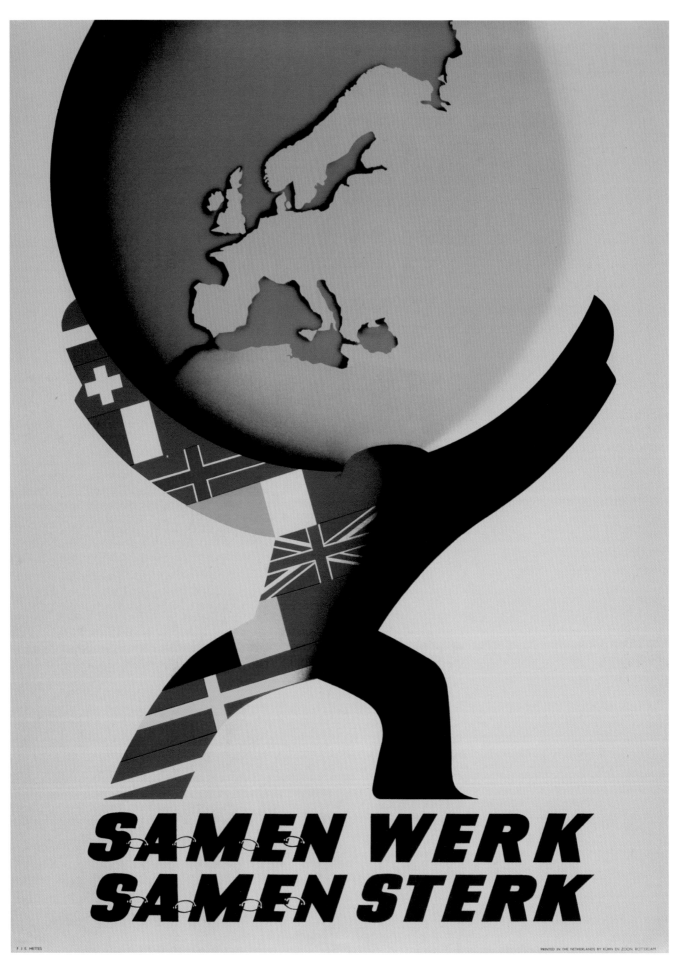

Plates 498-504, European Recovery Program
1950, 21½ × 29

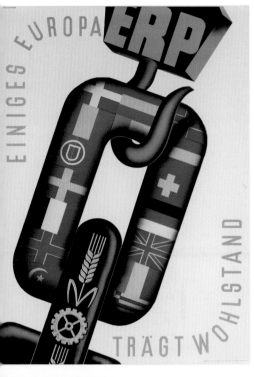

PLATE IDENTIFICATION:

All measurements are given in inches, width followed by height. When multiple sizes are known, all known sizes are listed. Additional sizes may exist. Under each photo of a poster is the size of the poster photographed; if additional sizes are known, the size is followed by *.

When an exact date is stated on the poster it is shown. When no date is given, the closest date based on reliable information is given as "ca. 19xx."

AMERICAN: RECRUITING

Plate 1 He Volunteered for Submarine Service. US Government Printing Office: 1944 -O- 566105 • Jon Witcomb, ca. 1944, 22 × 28

—————————————

Plate 2 Service Above Self, Medical Department, United States Army

Plate 3 Where Skill and Courage Count, Signal Corps, United States Army

Plate 4 Of the Troops and for the Troops, the Corps of Military Police, United States Army

Plate 5 O'er the Ramparts We Watch, United States Army Air Force.
War Department, Bureau of Public Relations, Brown & Bigelow, St. Paul, MN, USA • Jes Schlaikjer, 1942, 19 × 25
See also Plate 134, Schlaikjer's Women's Army Corps recruiting poster.

—————————————

Plate 6 Defend Your Country, Enlist Now in the United States Army, Spurgeon Tucker, New York, P-25 – 10-1-40–25M • Tom Woodburn, 1940, 9 × 12½ & 25 × 38

Plate 7 U.S. Army Guardian of the Colors Spurgeon Tucker, New York, P-9 – 10-1-40–25M • Tom Woodburn, 1940, 9 × 12½ & 25 × 38

Plate 8 U.S. Army, At Home Abroad • Tom Woodburn, 1940, 25 × 38

Plate 9 Defend Your Country, Enlist Now United States Army. Litho in USA, Spurgeon Tucker Litho., New York, NY 9-18-40-9500 • T.B.W. (Tom Woodburn), 1940, 59 × 46

Plate 10 Soldiers' Life, Make the Regular Army Your Career. P-30–RPB–4-15-41-25M • Tom Woodburn, 1941, 25 × 38

Plate 11 Remain with the Colors, Enlist in the Regular Army Reserve. PC-21–RPB–12-20-38–50M • Tom Woodburn, 1938, 9 × 13

Plate 12 Don't Gamble with Your Future, Pick a Sure Thing Now! US Army. P-217–RPB–8-15-45-50M • Graves, 1946, 25 × 38

Plate 13 I Want You for the U.S. Army. PC-43-RPB-1-2-41-100M • James Montgomery Flagg, 1941, 9 × 12½ & 25 × 38

Plate 14 Go Places with the U.S. Army. PC-, 20-RPB-10-25-40-100M • Anon., 1940, 25 × 38

Plate 15 Sports, the Army Builds Men. P-13-RPB-1-26-37-8m • Anon., 1937, 25 × 38

Plate 16 Vacancies Exist! Enlist Now. P-1-RPB-10-12-39-75 US Army • Anon., 1939, 25 × 38

Plate 17 Guard Our Shores, At Home and Abroad with the Coastal Artillery U.S. Army. P-23-RPB-8-23-40-12,500 • Anon.,1940, 25 × 38

Plate 18 West Point of the Air—Flying Cadets U.S. Army Air Corps. A.P-1-RPB-9-18-40-10M • Anon., 1940, 25 × 38

Plate 19 West Point of the Air—Flying Cadets U.S. Army Air Corps. RPB-4-15-39-4M-A-P-2 • Anon., 1939, 25 × 38

Plate 20 The Greatest Team in the World, AAF, Army Air Forces. P-X-54 RPB 7-11-44- 10M • Clayton Knight, 1944, 25 × 38

Plate 21 There's a Place for You on this Team! AAF, Army Air Forces. P-X-51 RPB 9-6-44- 10M • Clayton Knight, 1944, 25 × 38

Plate 22 Bombs Away! The Greatest Team in the World, AAF, Army Air Forces. P-X-62 RPB 9-9-44- 10M • CC Beall, 1944, 25 × 38

Plate 23 Wings Over America, Air Corps U.S. Army. P-21-RPB-9-18-40-25M • Tom Woodburn, 1940, 25 × 38

Plate 24 "Arise Americans" Your Country and Your Liberty Are in Grave Danger. Protect Them Now by Joining the—United States Navy or the U.S. Naval Reserve • McClelland Barclay, USNR, 1941, 27 × 41

Plate 25 Protect Your Future—Learn a Trade Apply U.S. Navy Recruiting Station • McClelland Barclay, USNR, 1941, 21 × 11

Plate 26 Fighting Fish and Fighting Men, Join up and Fight in the United States Navy • Anon., 1941, 20 × 14
The USS Pike was the first all-welded submarine, allowing for greater depths and protection from depth charge attacks.

Plate 27 Fight Let's Go! Join the Navy. NRB-31348 -1-20-42-15M • McClelland Barclay, USNR, 1942, 20 × 14

Plate 28 Contact! An enlistment in the U.S. Navy brings a young man into close contact with experience which will benefit him in later life. For information see U.S. Navy Recruiting Officer. NRB-18205-10-30-35-12,400 • Arthur Beaumont, 1935, 28 × 42

Plate 29 Join the Navy and (see) Free the World. NBR -31593-2-9-42-15M • M Privatello, 1942, 28 × 42

Plate 30 "Young Salts" Will You Carry On? Steel ships replace the wooden ones, steam has vanquished sail but the young men of Our Navy today carry on in the same spirit of zeal and faithfulness as the Old Salts of early days. NRB-16892-8-1-34-8M • Anon., 1934, 27 × 42

Plate 31 Dish it Out with the Navy, Choose now while you can — Go to your nearest Navy recruiting station today. NRB -35504-4-17-42- 125M • McClelland Barclay, USNR, 1942, 28 × 41

Plate 32 Naval Aviation has a Place for You.... Pilots, Machinist's Mates, Radiomen, Metalsmiths, Ordnancemen, Learn the right-way—the Navy-way, apply today • McClelland Barclay, USNR, ca. 1942, 28 × 41

Plate 33 Spearhead of Victory, Navy Day October 27. NAVPERS NRB-38674-24 SEP 43 -70M • John Falter, 1943, 26 × 37½

—————————————

Plate 34 Navy Blimps

Plate 35 Echelon-Avengers

Plate 36 Wave Spins the Props/The Dawn Comes up Like Thunder

Plate 37 Vought Corsair/Eyes of the Navy

Plate 38 Carrier Calisthenics/Better Men Than the Enemy

Plate 39 Baby Flat-Top
Aviation Training Division, Office of the Chief of the Naval Operations, Navy Dept., Wash DC • Edward J. Steichen (or naval photographic staff) ca. 1942, 39 × 59
Among the many works created by the Naval Aviation Photographic Unit under the command of Edward Steichen were a series of posters. The unit was created in 1942, in an effort to recruit pilots for the Navy, which was at the time in direct competition with the Army Air Force for able bodied young men.

———————————————

Plate 40 Your Job in the Navy, Enlist in the Navy Today. NRB-32669-6-10-42-25M • Anon., 1942, 28 × 42

Plate 41 Sub Spotted-Let 'Em Have It! Lend a Hand—Enlist in Your Navy Today • McClelland Barclay, USNR, ca. 1942, 28 × 42

Plate 42 Let's Hit 'Em With Everything We've Got! Don't Wait—Choose the Navy. Order No.1, Lutz and Shenkman-33249 -4-25-42-125M • McClelland Barclay, USNR, 1942, 28 × 42,

Plate 43 United States Navy needs young Patriotic Americans to man its expanding fleet. Opportunities are offered for service in every branch. Apply Now! NRB-28151-10-1-40-10M • Matt Murphey, USN, 1940, 28 × 42

Plate 44 Help Keep It Great! Freshmen! Sophomores! Stay in college and become a Naval Officer. NRB-32620-6-3-42-15M • Anon., 1942, 28 × 42

Plate 45 Enemy Sighted—Attack! Lend a Hand—Enlist in the Navy Today. NRB – 33070–7-31-42–10M • John Philip Falter, USN, 1942, 28 × 42

Plate 46 Train Today, While you Fight for Tomorrow, Learn Diesels with the Submarine Service. U.S. Government Printing Office 1944-O -566105 • Anon., 1944, 18 × 24

Plate 47 Smack the Japs! Volunteer for Submarine Service. US Government Printing Office 1944-O -566105 • Anon.,1944, 22 × 28

Plate 48 Construction Workers! Now you can volunteer for service in the Army or Navy. Use your trade skills to fight with the Navy Seabees Army Engineers. P-59-RPB-3-30-43-35M • Dan v. Smith, 1943, 25 × 38

Plate 49 Build for Your Navy! Seabees, Enlist Carpenters, Machinists, Electricians, Etc., Seabees • R Muchley, ca. 1942, 14 × 22

Plate 50 Construction Workers! Now you can volunteer for service with the Army or Navy. Work and fight Navy Seabees Army Engineers. P-60-RPB-4-10-43-50M • S.G. (initials),1943, 25 × 38

Plate 51 Construction Workers... Build and fight for Victory—Join the Seabees. NRB-35900 – 5-12-43– 93M • John Falter USNR, 1943, 14 × 22 & 25 × 38

Plate 52 The U.S. Marines Want You. MCRB 104890 -9-2-42 10M, 436 PB • Anon., 1942, 28 × 38½

Plate 53 Ready, Join U.S. Marines, Land Air Sea. REQN No 1546 5-26-42 25M, 436 PB, Alpha Litho Co. Camden, NJ • Haddon Sundblom, 1942, 28 × 40

Plate 54 On to Victory with the U.S. Marines. MCPB 106354 9-29-42 20M, 433 PB • Anon., 1942, 11 × 14

Plate 55 Wear the Fightin'est wings in the service, Fly with the Marines. NOM 3667 10-2-42 15M, 436 PB • HHL (initials), 1942, 28 × 40

Plate 56 U.S. Marines, Soldiers Who Go to Sea. MCPB 106353 9-29-42 20M 433PB • Anon., 1942, 11 × 14

Plate 57 This Device on Headgear or Uniform Means U.S. Marines. MCPB 106352 9-29-42 20M 433 PB • Anon., 1942, 11 × 14

Plate 58 U.S. Marines Deliver the Goods Too • Vic Guinness U.S.M.C., ca. 1942, 58½ × 45½

Plate 59 Land with the U.S. Marines. 9-17-42 REQN No 2118 10M, Litho in the USA McCandlish Litho Corporation Philadelphia, PA • Vic Guinness U.S.M.C., 1942, 28 × 40

Plate 60 Let's Go Get 'Em! U.S. Marines Polygraphic Co of America, Inc New York 8-12-42, 436 PB 15M • Vic Guinness Captain U.S.M.C., 1942, 11 × 14 & 28 × 40

Plate 61 Hit Hard and Often with the Marines. Mc Candlish Litho Corporation, Phila, PA, 8-12-42, 15M • Anon., 1942, 11 × 14 & 28 × 40

Plate 62 U.S. Marines on LAND at SEA in the AIR, Defend America. MCFP 10-9-41 5M • Anon., 1941, 30 × 40
This poster was reprinted in 1942, with the sole change being the addition of the word "NOW!" below the map of the United States.

Plate 63 Always Advance with the U.S. Marines, Land, Sea, Air, 1775 1942, 167th Anniversary. 9-18-42 Req'n No 1603 100M, Litho in U.S.A. McCandlish Litho Corporation, Phila. PA. • Anon., 1942, 28 × 22

Plate 64 "The Marines Have Landed", Apply To Nearest Recruiting Station. Alpha Lithograph Co, Camden NJ. 9-10-42 15M, 436 PB • James Montgomery Flagg, 1942, 30 × 40
This poster was first printed on 12/12/1941, just days after the attack on Pearl Harbor.

Plate 65 Want Action? Join U.S. Marine Corps! Apply to Nearest Recruiting Station. 10M–436PB, Alpha Lithograph Co., Camden N.J. 6-3-42 • James Montgomery Flagg, 1942, 30 × 40

Plate 66 Always Ready Join Today U.S. Coast Guard, Remember Pearl Harbor. CGTC-No3V • Anon., ca. 1942, 22 × 28
Semper Paratus—Always Ready is the Coast Guard motto.

Plate 67 Clear for Action U.S. Coast Guard. 10-43 Graphic Arts Unit U.S.C.G. • Anon., 1943, 28 × 42

Plate 68 Every Minute Counts, Remember .. there's no quitting time on the Fighting Fronts! U.S. Coast Guard • Anon., ca. 1942, 22 × 28

Plate 69, Blast 'Em with the Sub-Busters, U.S. Coast Guard NRB-34631-1-12-43-25M • Anon., 1943, 21 × 11,

Plate 70 Defend your Country, Serve with the U.S. Coast Guard NRB-29757-7-8-41-25M • Anon., 1941, 21 × 11

Plate 71 On Watch! Enlist Today, U.S. Coast Guard, 7-43, Graphic Arts Unit U.S.C.G. • Anon., 1943, 14 × 19

Plate 72 Good Hunting with the U.S. Coast Guard, Join Today, Graphic Arts Unit U.S.C.G, 2-43 • Anon., 1943, 14 × 19
See also Plates 227, 304, 391 & 445.

Plate 73 Go Higher, Farther, Faster, U.S. Air Force. P-253-RPB–5-15-48–70M • Richard Tobin, 1948, 24 × 37

Plate 74 A Career in the Air Awaits You, U.S. Air Force. P249-RPB-4-15-48-70M • Anon., 1948, 24 × 36

Plate 75 Only the Best Can Be Aviation Cadets, U.S.Air Force. PX 118-RPB-8-10-48-50M • Anon., 1948, 24 × 36

Plate 76 United States Air Force, Air Power Is Peace Power. PX-114-RPB-4-25-48-50M • Anon., 1948, 25 × 38

HEALTH & PERSONAL HYGIENE

Plate 77 Keep Fit to Fight. First Air Force Physical Fitness Poster No 3, Designed & Reproduced by F.A.F. AV Engr Repro Detach • Del Cimmuto., ca. 1942, 14 × 19½
The "First Air Force," a unit of the Army, was one of the original four numbered air forces. During WWII, it was charged with regional responsibility to provide defense of the northeast and Great Lakes regions.

Plate 78 It's an Old American Custom, Keep Clean, Take a bath every day you can. • Anon., ca. 1944, 14 × 20

Plate 79 Keep Your Shirt on Soldier, Exposed Skin After Dark is Meat for the Malaria Mosquito, Fight the Peril behind the Lines. U.S. Government Printing Office 1943-O-564971 • Anon., 1943, 14 × 17

Plate 80 Don't Let Lice Make a Monkey out of You! U.S. Government Printing Office 1944- O-691222 • Vernon Grant, 1944, 14 × 20

Plate 81 Protection in a Bottle, Use Your Insect Repellent as Directed! Fight the Peril behind the Lines. U.S. Government Printing Office: 1944-O-574718 • Frank Bensing, 1944, 14 × 17

Plate 82 Net Profit, It Pays to Use Your Bed Net—Avoid Malaria. U.S. Government Printing Office: 1946-O-703233 • Anon., 1946, 13 × 18½

Plate 83 His Mask—U.S. Government Printing Office: 1942-O-460435

Plate 84 Dental Care—U.S. Government Printing Office: 1942-O-045813

Plate 85 Clean Dry Clothes—U.S. Government Printing Office: 1942-O-460435

Plate 86 Foods that Count—U.S. Government Printing Office: 1942-O-460435

Plate 87 Fun, off the Job—U.S. Government Printing Office: 1942-O-460435

Plate 88 Plenty of Sleep—U.S. Government Printing Office: 1942-O-485813

Plate 89 Regular Check Ups—U.S. Government Printing Office: 1942-O-460435
Federal Security Agency U.S. Public Health Service Keep Him on the Job. • H. Price, 1942, 9½ × 12½
See also female companion posters "Jenny on the Job" Plates 150-156.

Plate 90 VD Can Wreck a Lot of Plans. VDgraphics 106 • Anon., ca. 1945, 15 × 20

Plate 91 Syphilis, a Million New Victims Each Year. United States Public Health Service • Anon., ca. 1942, 15 × 20

Plate 92 Go Back to Civvies Clean, Guard Against Venereal Disease. VDgraphic-34 • Anon., ca. 1944, 15 × 20

Plate 93 VD, a Sorry Ending to a Furlough, Prophylaxis Prevents Venereal Disease! VDgraphic -76 • Ferree, ca. 1945, 16 × 21

Plate 94 The New Pro Kit, Simple, Easy, Effective. Always Use Soap and Water First, Cpl. Emax. • Anon., ca. 1942, 11 × 14

Plate 95 VD Can Wreck a Lot of Plans, but Prophylaxis Prevents VD. • Anon., ca. 1942, 16 × 19

Plate 96 VD May Ruin Your Career. U.S. Government Printing Office: 767229, USN Navpers 110051 VD 6 • Anon., ca. 1942, 15 × 20,

Plate 97 Furlough "Booby Trap!", No Is the Best Tactic; the Next, PROphylactic! ASCPG-8 • Anon., ca. 1944, 14 × 18½

Plate 98 There's Nothing New Under the Sun ... including the VD She Can Give You! NavMed 990, VP-28, Bureau of Medicine and Surgery, U.S. Navy, U.S. Government Printing Office 1946 O-683664 Prepared in cooperation with the U.S. Naval Medical School, National Naval Medical Center, Bethesda, Md. • Bode, 1946, 18 × 26

Plate 99 "A Sailor Doesn't Have to Prove He's a Man!" Remember: There's No Medicine for Regret. U.S. Government Printing Office: 1945-O-659038 • Bode, 1945, 18½ × 25½

Plate 100 If You Must Be a Dumb Bunny Stay One Jump Ahead of Trouble! U.S. Government Printing Office: 1945-O-659039 • Bode, 1945, 18½ × 25½

Plate 101 Juke Joint Sniper, Syphilis and Gonorrhea.

VDgraphics-25 • Ferree, ca. 1944, 15 × 20

Plate 102 Booby Trap, Syphilis and Gonorrhea. VDgraphics-52 • Ferree, ca. 1944, 15 × 20

Plate 103 V-E V-J, There Is an Enemy Still to Be Defeated, VD. Anon., ca. 1945, 60 × 46

Plate 104 Most Promiscuous Women Have Venereal Disease, Don't Take a chance, Take a Pro. V.D.5, Distributed through the medical department, U.S.A. S.O.S. S.W.P.A. '44 • SGT Epstein (Ralph Epstein), 1944, 14 × 22
United States Army Services of Supply, Southwest Pacific Area (USA SOS SWPA).

Plate 105 Both of These Men Had Syphilis—He took His Syphilis Shots Every Week until Cured, He Didn't Take His Shots. VDgraphics -7 • Karsakow + Ferree, ca. 1941, 20 × 28

Plate 106 Venereal Disease Covers the Earth, Learn to Protect Yourself Now. VDgraphics-42 • F. Williams, ca. 1942, 15 × 25

Plate 107 Don't Pick It Up! U.S. Government Printing Office: 1945-O-785112, Navpers 110051 VD-8 • Anon., 1948, 15 × 20

Plate 108 Easy to Get, Syphilis and Gonorrhea. U.S. Government Printing Office: 1943-O -511293 • (signature unintelligible). 1943, 14 × 20

Plate 109 Easy to Get, Syphilis and Gonorrhea, Don't Take a Chance, Take a Pro. V.D.4, Distributed through the medical department, U.S.A. S.O.S. '44 • SGT Epstein (Ralph Epstein), 1943, 14 × 22
Sign in window in background reads "U.S. Army Prophylactic Station."

Plate 110 Bright Future Ahead! Steer Clear of VD. U.S. Government Printing Office: 1948-O -809278, NAVPERS 110051 VD-13 • Anon., 1948, 14 × 18

WAR BONDS AND STAMPS

Plate 111 Buy War Bonds. U.S. Government Printing Office: 1942-O-474689 WSS 510-A • N. C. Wyeth, 1942, 11 × 14, 14 × 22, 20 × 28, 28 × 40, 30 × 40, & 40 × 60

Plate 112 Our Good Earth ...Keep It Ours, Buy War Bonds "Make Every Market Day Bond Day." U.S. Government Printing Office: 1942-O-472529 WSS 509-B • John Steuart Curry, 1942, 16 × 22½ & 40 × 60

Plate 113 Buy a Share in America. United States Defense Bonds, Ask about Our Pay Roll Savings Purchase Plan. U.S. Government Printing Office: 1941-O-417820 • John C. Atherton, 1941, 9½ × 13½ & 41½ × 56

Plate 114 Hasten the Homecoming, Buy Victory Bonds. From the *Saturday Evening Post* Cover Painting • Norman Rockwell, ca. 1945, 20 × 29 *See also* Saturday Evening Post *companion advertising posters Plates 358-359.*

Plate 115 Freedom from Fear, O.W.I. Poster No. 46, U.S. Government Printing Office: 1943-O-511887

Plate 116 Freedom from Want, O.W.I. Poster No. 45, U.S. Government Printing Office: 1943-O-511886

Plate 117 Freedom of Worship, O.W.I. Poster No. 43, U.S. Government Printing Office: 1943-O-510256

Plate 118 Freedom of Speech, O.W.I. Poster No. 44, U.S. Government Printing Office: 1943-O-510257 The Four Freedoms. • Norman Rockwell, 1943, 20 × 28, 28 × 40 & 40 × 56

Plate 119 Don't Let That Shadow Touch Them, Buy War Bonds. U.S. Government Printing Office: 1942-O-462211 WSS 451-A • Anon., 1942, 28 × 40

Plate 120 "Deliver Us from Evil" Buy War Bonds, Official U.S. Treasury Poster. U.S. Government Printing Office: 1943-O-523825 WSS 808 • Anon., 1943, 8½ × 11, 20 × 28, & 28 × 40

Plate 121 At Ticket Windows Where You See This Emblem, Buy Defense Savings Stamps Here, a Service of the American Railroads in the Interest of National Defense. 16-21883a U.S. Government Printing Office 1941 • Anon., 1941, 22 × 28

Plate 122 Let's Fly This Flag, Everybody at Least 10% in War Bonds. U.S. Government Printing Office: 1942-O-476088 WSS551 • Anon., 1942, 22 × 28

Plate 123 For Victory... Put at Least 10% of Every Pay into War Bonds! • Anon., 1942, 17 × 22

Plate 124 Just Be Sure You Put at Least 10% of It in War Bonds!, Top That 10%. U.S. Government Printing Office 1942-O-496667 WSS 694 • Anon., 1942, 22 × 28 *See also Plate 478.*

Plate 125 Attack Attack Attack, Buy War Bonds. U.S. Government Printing Office 1942-O-497775

WSS 697-C • Ferdinand Warren, 1942, 22 × 28 & 28 × 40

Plate 126 "You Buy 'Em, We'll Fly 'Em!" Defense Bonds Stamps. U.S. Government Printing Office 1942-O-436100 • Wilkinson, 1942, 10 × 14, 20 × 28 & 40 × 60

Plate 127 Till We Meet Again, Buy War Bonds. U.S. Government Printing Office 1942-O-491739 WSS 645-C • Joseph Hirsch, 1942, 16 × 22 & 40 × 60

Plate 128 For Their Future—Buy War Bonds. U.S. Government Printing Office 1943-O-513138 WSS 776-A • Munsell, 1943, 28 × 40

Plate 129 "Even a Little Can Help a Lot-Now", Buy U.S. War Stamps Bonds. U.S. Government Printing Office 1942-O-455803 FORM DSS-405, Illustration Courtesy of *Ladies' Home Journal* • A Parker, 1942, 14 × 20

Plate 130 We Can... We Will.. We Must! Franklin D. Roosevelt, Buy U.S. War Savings Bonds & Stamps Now. U.S. Government Printing Office 1942-O-453557 Form DSS-355 • Anon., 1942, 20½ × 11

Plate 131 Buy That Invasion Bond! U.S. Government Printing Office 1942-O-597754 FORM DSS-405 • R. Moore, 1944, 40 × 28

Plate 132 Jap... You're Next! Buy Extra Bonds. P-X-63-RPB-5-6-45-150M • James Montgomery Flagg, 1945, 14 × 20 & 20 × 28

Plate 133 7th War Loan Now—All Together. U.S. Government Printing Office 1945-O-637960 WFD 11A, Official U. S. Treasury Poster, U.S. Marines at Iwo Jima, Painted By C.C. Beall From Associated Press Photo • C C Beall, 1945, 9 × 12½, 18½ × 25 & 26 × 37 *Based on 1945 Pulitzer Prize winning photograph "Raising the Flag in Iwo Jima" by Joe Rosenthal.*

WOMEN AT WAR

Plate 134 Mine Eyes Have Seen the Glory, Women's Army Corp, Army of the United States. P-X-53-RPB 5-2-44- 850M • Jes Schlaikjer, 1944, 20 × 28 *See also Plates 2-5 Schlaikjer Army recruiting posters.*

Plate 135 Women There's Work to Be Done and a War to Be Won...Now! See Your U.S. Employment Service, War Manpower Commission. U.S. Government Printing Office 1944-O-598047 • Vernon Grant for O.W.I., 1944, 14 × 20 & 21 × 11

Plate 136 "The Girl He Left Behind" Is Still Behind Him, She's a WOW, Woman Ordnance Worker. Ordnance Department U.S. Army Keep 'Em Shooting! • Adolph Treidler, 1943, 27 × 42

Plate 137 She's a WOW, Woman Ordnance Worker. Government Printing Office 1942-O-498370, Ordnance Department U.S. Army Keep Em Shooting! • Adolph Treidler, 1942, 27 × 42

Plate 138 Enlist in a Proud Profession! Join the U.S. Cadet Nurse Corps, A Lifetime Education FREE! If You can Qualify. U.S. Public Health Service, Federal Security Agency • Edmundson, ca. 1942, 20 × 28

Plate 139 You Are Needed Now, Join the Army Nurse Corps. "poster 710-A" June 1943 • Ruzzie Green, 1943, 20½ × 31

Plate 140 Enlist in a Proud Profession ... Join the U.S. Cadet Nurse Corp, A Lifetime Education FREE! For High School Graduates Who Qualify. Distributed by OWI for the Federal Security Agency, U.S. Public Health Service, Federal Security Agency, U.S. Government Printing Office 1943-O-562744 • Anon., 1943, 20 × 28

Plate 141 Become a Nurse. Your Country Needs You, Write Nursing Information Bureau, 1790 Broadway, New York City. U.S. Government Printing Office: 1942-O-453124, Federal Security Agency-U.S. Public Health Service • Anon., 1942, 14 × 20 & 20 × 28

Plate 142 Enlist in the WAVES, Release a Man to Fight at Sea. Order No 19, NRB -34694-1-13-43-40M • Anon., 1943, 28 × 42

Plate 143 "Join Up with Us" Be an Army Air-WAC Keep Us Flying. P.R.O. A.A.F W.T.T.C. REPROD LF • Heller, ca. 1944, 19½ × 28 *The Western Technical Training Command, Denver, Colorado, was established as a unit of the Army Air Force Nov. 1,1941, and inactivated October 15, 1945.*

Plate 144 Share the Deeds of Victory, Join the Waves. NAVPERS NRB-38070-10 AUG 43 140M • John Philip Falter, USNR, 1943, 28 × 42

Plate 145 Women Work for Victory, Farm Office Factory, Apply Nearest U.S. Employment Service Office or State Defense Council, Hartford. A Conn. WPA Poster • Anon., ca. 1942, 18 × 26

Plate 146 "The Girl of the Year Is a SPAR", Enlist in the Coast Guard Spars, Apply Nearest Coast Guard Office. • WT Bentley, 1942, 28 × 42

Plate 147 Be a Marine, Free a Marine to Fight. Cont. NOm-42757 335000, Distributed by OWI for the U.S. Marines Corps, McCandlish Litho Corporation Phila Pa • Anon., 1942, 14 × 22

Plate 148 "Proud—I'll Say" Join the WAVES. Burpers-NRB-36962-31 July 43-40M • John Falter USNR, 1943, 28 × 42

Plate 149 Join Women's Land Army of the U.S. Crop Corps. U.S. Government Printing Office: 1943-O-534295 • Morley, 1943, 20 × 28

———————————

Plate 150 Steps ahead with Low Heels WH 15

Plate 151 Gets Her Beauty Sleep WH 12

Plate 152 Lifts Weight the Easy Way WH 16

Plate 153 Eats Man Size Meals WH 11

Plate 154 Has Her Fun after Work WH 14

Plate 155 Let's Keep OUR Restroom Clean! WH 17

Plate 156 Keeps Fresh as a Daisy, WH 13
Jenny on the Job. Federal Security Agency U.S. Public Health Service, U.S.Government Printing Office: 1943-O-529958 • Kula, 1943, 10 × 14
See also male companion posters Keep Him on the Job Plates 83-89.

———————————

Plate 157 I'll Carry Mine Too! Trucks and tires must last till victory. OWI Poster No 28, U.S.Government Printing Office: 1943-O-503155, Office of Defense Transportation • Sarra, 1943, 22 × 28

Plate 158 "Of Course I Can! I'm Patriotic as Can Be—And Ration Points Won't Worry Me!" Distributed by OWI for WFA, U.S. Government Printing Office 1944-O-643470 • Dick Williams, 1944, 18 × 25

MINORITY EXPERIENCE

Plate 159 Twice a Patriot! Ex-Private Obie Bartlett Lost Left Arm-Pearl Harbor- Released: Dec., 1942- Now at Work Welding in a West Coast Shipyard...

"Sometimes I feel My Job Here Is as Important as the One I Had to Leave". U.S. Government Printing Office: 1943-O -535256 WPB Poster No.A- 17 • Anon., 1943, 28 × 40

Plate 160 United We Win. U.S. Government Printing Office: 1942-O -484339, War Manpower Commission Washington, D.C. • Liberman, 1942, 20 × 28 & 28 × 40

Plate 161 Pvt. Joe Louis Says "We're Going to Do Our Part ... and We'll Win because We're on God's Side". U.S. Government Printing Office: 1942-O • Anon., 1942, 7 × 10 & 17½ × 25

Plate 162 Build for the Future, "without vision there is no hope. Protect your country...and your future", George Washington Carver, Buy Victory Bonds WFD 61 U.S. Government Printing Office: 1945-O 666820 Official U.S. Treasury Poster • Kautz, 1945, 18½ × 25

Plate 163 "Above and Beyond the Call of Duty" Dorie Miller Received the Navy Cross at Pearl Harbor, May 27, 1943. OWI Poster No 68, U. S. Government Printing Office 1943-O-530929 • David Stone Martin, 1943, 20 × 28
Doris (Dorie) Miller, a cook in the United States Navy was noted for his bravery during the attack on Pearl Harbor in 1941. He was the first African American to be awarded the Navy Cross.

Plate 164 Keep Us Flying! Buy War Bonds. U. S. Government Printing Office: 1943-O -560778, Official U.S. Treasury Poster, WFD 874 • Anon., 1943, 22 × 28
Identity of the proud Tuskegee Airman in this poster is unconfirmed, but most often cited as Lt. Robert W. Diez.

Plate 165 Libres (The 4 Freedoms). Publicado por el Coordinador de Asuntos Interamericanos, Washington, E.U.A. • Herbert Bayer, ca. 1942, 20 × 28

Plate 166 Americanos Todos Luchamos Por La Victoria, Americans All, Let's Fight For Victory. OWI Poster No. 65, U.S. Government Printing Office: 1943-O 528719 • Leon Helguera, 1943, 22 × 26

Plate 167 Western Defense Command and Fourth Army, Wartime Civil Control Administration, Presidio of San Francisco California April 24 1942 Instructions to all Persons of Japanese Ancestry • Anon., 1942, 8½ × 14

Plate 168 No loyal citizen of the United States should be denied the democratic right to exercise the responsibilities of his citizenship, regardless of his ancestry. The principle on which this country was founded and by which it has always been governed is that Americanism is a matter of the

mind and heart; "Americanism is not, and never was, a matter of race or ancestry". OWI Poster No 75., U.S. Government Printing Office: 1943-O 533582 • Anon., 1943, 20 × 28
Less than ten months had elapsed between the internment of Japanese Americans mandated in Plate 167 and Franklin D. Roosevelt's speech announcing the formation of the 442nd Infantry Regiment quoted in Plate 168. While the unit was almost entirely made up of Japanese Americans, the vast majority of its volunteers came from Hawaii, where internment did not occur, rather than from Japanese Americans living on the mainland of the United States where internment was mandatory.

CONSERVATION

Plate 169 Plant a Victory Garden, Our Food Is Fighting, A Garden Will Make Your Rations Go Further. O.W.I. Poster No 34, U.S. Government Printing Office: 1942-O-506017 • Anon., 1942, 22 × 28

Plate 170 Your Victory Garden Counts More Than Ever! War Food Administration, U.S. Government Printing Office: 1945-O-629743 • Morley, 1945, 19 × 26½

Plate 171 Can All You Can. O.W.I. Poster No 77, U.S. Government Printing Office: 1943-O 533993 • Anon., 1943, 16 × 22 1/5

Plate 172 U.S. Needs Us Strong, Eat Nutritional Food. Office of Defense Health and Welfare Services, Washington, D.C. • Anon., ca. 1942, 13 × 20

Plate 173 Get in the Scrap, Aerial Bomb, Medium Tank, Battleship, Anti-Aircraft Gun. U.S. Government Printing Office 1942-O-471153, War Production Board, Bureau of Industrial Conservation • Anon., 1942, 22 × 28

Plate 174 America Needs Your Scrap Rubber, Gas Mask, Life Raft, Scout Car, Heavy Bomber. U.S. Government Printing Office 1942-O-469847, War Production Board, Bureau of Industrial Conservation • Anon., 1942, 22 × 28

Plate 175 Win with Tin. U.S. Government Printing Office 1942-O-469307, War Production Board, Bureau of Industrial Conservation • Anon., 1942, 22 × 28

Plate 176 Save Waste Fats for Explosives, Take Them to Your Meat Dealer. O.W.I Poster No.63, U.S. Government Printing Office: 1943- O-527285 • Koener, 1943, 18 × 22 & 20 × 28

Plate 177 For Victory—And My Personal Post War World, I'm Following the 7-Key Plan to Hold Prices Down.

Plate 178 Here's How to Head Off Runaway Prices, Follow the 7-Key Plan to Hold Prices Down

Plate 179 I'm Out to Lick Runaway Prices, Lets All Follow the 7-Key Plan to Hold Prices Down. VICTORY
1 Buy and hold war bond.
2 Pay willingly our share of taxes.
3 Provide adequate life insurance and savings for our future.
4 Reduce our debts as much as possible.
5 Buy only what we need and make what we have last longer.
6 Follow ration rules and price ceilings.
7 Cooperate with our Government's wage stabilization program.
Distributed by O.W.I. for the Office of Economic Stabilization. • Anon., ca. 1942, 20 × 28

Plate 180 Defense Needs Rubber, Save Your Tires. Division of Information, Office for Emergency Management, U.S. Government Printing Office 1941-0 419307 • Anon., 1941, 28 × 40

Plate 181 Today Every Fire Helps Hitler, Fire Prevention Week. National Fire Prevention Association, Boston, Mass -Printed in U.S.A. • Anon., 1942, 12 × 16

Plate 182 Strike Down This Monster! Forest Fires Delay Victory. Department of Agriculture Poster • Anon., 1942, 14 × 18

Plate 183 Our Carelessness, Their Secret Weapon, Prevent Forest Fires. U.S. Dept. of Agriculture Forest Services, State of Wisconsin Conservation Department, U.S. Government Printing Office 1943-0 505840 • Anon., 1943, 22 × 28

Plate 184 Careless Matches Aid the Axis, Prevent Forest Fires! U.S. Government Printing Office 1942-O-468267 • Anon., 1942, 18 × 24 & 38 × 50

Plate 185 Have You Really Tried to Save Gas by Getting into a Car Club? U.S. Government Printing Office 1944-O-585265 • Harold Von Schmidt, 1944, 20 × 28 & 28 × 40

Plate 186 Is Your Trip Necessary? Needless Travel Interferes with the War Effort, Office of Defense Transportation. O.W.I. Poster No. 74., U.S. Government Printing Office 1943-0 533555 • Anon., 1943, 20 × 28

Plate 187 Me Travel? ...Not This Summer, Vacation at Home. Office of Defense Transportation • Albert Dorne, 1945, 20 × 28 & 26 × 37

Plate 188 When You Ride Alone, You Ride with Hitler! U.S. Government Printing Office: 1943-O-538876 • Weimer Pursell, 1943, 20 × 28

Plate 189 Clear the Tracks for War Shipments, Buy Coal Now! Division of Information, Office for Emergency Management, Washington, D.C. • Anon., ca. 1942, 28 × 20

Plate 190 Don't Shiver Next Winter, Order Coal Now, Solid Fuels Administration for War, Washington, D.C. U.S. Government Printing Office: 1944-O-641974 • Arens, 1944, 18½ × 26

TRAINING FOR THE MISSION

Plate 191 Hit That Target! Poster No. 1209 9/42

Plate 192 Target Destroyed, Poster No. 1211 9/42

Plate 193 Precision Teamwork Means Precision Bombing, Poster No. 1207 9/42

Plate 194 Precision Training Means Precision Bombing, Poster No. 1208 9/42
Precision Bombing. Aircraft Identification Section DIT-AAF • Anon., 1942, 18 × 25

Plates 195-204 Recognition Tests. Bureau of Naval Personnel, Nav Pers 20108 • Anon., 1943, 11 × 14
Shown are 10 examples for over 25 different training posters each showing a profile of Allied aircraft and Axis aircraft. Revealed under the flap marked "Answer" is information about the airplanes shown.

Plate 205-214 Rules of the Road, Running Lights, AVA DEPT. USNTS SAMPSON, N.Y. • Anon., ca. 1943, 11½ × 14

Shown are ten posters from a set of twenty-three nautical training posters created for use at United States Naval Training Station Sampson. Established in 1942 and closed in 1946, the station in upstate New York provided basic training to over 400,000 recruits during the war.

Plates 215-224 untitled (Naval flag training charts) • Anon., ca. 1943, 11½ × 14
Shown are ten posters from a set of training posters including the full alphabet, numbers, and specialized nautical signals.

CARELESS TALK

Plate 225 Loose Talk Can Cost Lives Distributed in the interest of national defense and as a means of obtaining funds for ambulances wherever needed. British and American Ambulance Corps, Inc, 420 Lexington Avenue, New York City. • W. Steig, 1942, 14 × 22

Plate 226 Button Your Lip, Loose Talk Can Cost Lives. Distributed in the interest of national defense and as a means of obtaining funds for ambulances wherever needed. British and American Ambulance Corps, Inc, 420 Lexington Avenue, New York City. • O Soglow, 1942, 14 × 22

Plate 227 Loose talk can cost lives. Distributed in the interest of national defense and as a means of obtaining funds for ambulances wherever needed. British and American Ambulance Corps, Inc, 420 Lexington Avenue, New York City. • Stevan Dohanos, 1942, 14 × 22
See also Plates 72, 304, 391, & 445.

Plate 228 Silence Means Surprise. W.D., A.G.O., "Surprise" Security Poster • Anon., 1943, 14½ × 22½

Plate 229 ...Because Somebody Talked. U.S. Government Printing Office: 1944-O -579038 • Wesley Heyman, 1944, 14 × 20 & 20 × 28
On the wall behind the cocker spaniel hangs a "Gold Star" service flag representing a family member who has died in the service of the United States.

Plate 230 Award for Careless Talk, Don't Discuss Troop Movements—Ship Sailings—War Equipment. U.S. Government Printing Office: 1944-O -602587 • Stevan Dohanos, 1944, 20 × 26 & 28 × 40

Plate 231 Wanted! For Murder, Her Careless Talk Cost Lives. U.S. Government Printing Office: 1944-O -556600 • Victor Keppler, 1944, 20 × 28 & 28 × 40

Plate 232 Someone Talked! OWI Poster No. 18, U.S. Government Printing Office: 1944-O -496733 • Siebel, 1944, 28 × 40

Plate 233 Bits of Careless Talk Are Pieced Together by the Enemy. U.S. Government Printing Office: 1943-O -563414, Distributed by OWI for the issuing agencies. • Stevan Dohanos, 1943, 20 × 28 & 28 × 40

Plate 234 Enemy Ears Are Listening. OWI No. 5, U.S. Government Printing Office: 1942-O -480485 • Anon., 1942, 26 × 13½

Plate 235 Careless Talk ...Got There First. U.S. Government Printing Office: 1944-O -593271 • Herbert Morton Stoops, 1944, 20 × 28 & 28 × 40

Plate 236 I'm Counting on You! Don't Discuss-Troop Movements, Ship Sailings, War Equipment. OWI Poster No 78, U.S. Government Printing Office: 1943-O -534057 • L Helguera, 1943, 20 × 28 & 28 × 40

Plate 237 If You Tell Where He's Going... He may Never Get There! U.S. Government Printing Office: 1943-O -556153 • John Falter, USNR, 1943, 20 × 28 & 28 × 40

Plate 238 Less Dangerous Than Careless Talk, Don't Discuss Troop Movements, Ship Sailings, War Equipment. U.S. Government Printing Office: 1944-O -603532 • Albert Dorne, 1944, 28 × 40

Plate 239 If You Tell Where They're Going, They May Never Get There. U.S. Government Printing Office: 1943-O-519564 • Anon., 1943, 28 × 40

Plate 240 A Careless Word ... a Needless Loss. U.S. Government Printing Office: 1943-O -506018 • Anton Otto Fisher, 1943, 22 × 28 & 28 × 40

Plate 241 We Caught Hell!—Someone Must Have Talked. U.S. Government Printing Office 1944-O-567525 • Saul Tepper, 1944, 28 × 40

Plate 242 He's Watching You. U.S. Government Printing Office 1942-O-455330 • Grobe, 1942, 10 × 14½ & 28 × 40
The Stahlhelm M16 steel helmet was an icon of the German military power to the Axis and a symbol of evil to the Allies.

PRODUCTION

Plate 243 Give 'Em Both Barrels. Division of Information for Emergency Management, Washington, D.C., U.S. Government Printing Office: 1941-O -430380 • Jean Carlu, 1941, 20 × 15 & 40 × 30

Plate 244 America's Answer! Production. U.S. Government Printing Office: 1942-O -454042, Division of Information for Emergency Management, Washington, D.C. • Jean Carlu, 1942, 40 × 30

Plate 245 Don't Let Him Down! Division of Information, Office for Emergency Management, Washington, D.C. • Lester Beall, 1941, 30 × 40

Plate 246 Give It Your Best! Office of War Information, Poster No. 9, U.S. Government Printing Office: 1942-O -488228 • Charles T Coiner, 1942, 20 × 15, 28 × 20, 40 × 28, & 56 × 40

Plate 247 Keep 'Em Rolling! Division of Information, Office for Emergency Management, Washington, D.C., U.S. Government Printing Office: 1941 • Leo Lionni, 1941, 30 × 40

Plate 248 Keep 'Em Rolling! Division of Information, Office for Emergency Management, Washington, D.C., U.S. Government Printing Office: 1941 • Leo Lionni, 1941, 30 × 40
Lionni created four Keep 'Em Rolling posters—PT Boats, tanks, anti-aircraft guns, and fighter aircraft — each using the motif of the American flag as a background.

Plate 249 Next Stop Tokyo—Let's Go!, Can I Tell 'em You're Still with Us? Official Navy Poster, Industrial Incentive Division, 11-80M, U.S. Government Printing Office 1945-O-632712 • John Falter USNR, 1945, 28 × 42

Plate 250 Full Speed Ahead, We've Still Got a Big Job to Do!, Couldn't Have Done it without You! Official Navy Poster, Industrial Incentive Division, 2-80M, U.S. Government Printing Office 1943-O-551620 • Howard Scott, 1943, 28 × 42

Plate 251 Pour It On! United States War Production Board, U.S. Government Printing Office 1942-O-476539 • Garrett Price, 1942, 7 × 10, 28½ × 40½

Plate 252 Let's Give Him Enough and on Time. U.S. Government Printing Office 1942-O-468088, Ordnance Department, U.S. Army Keep 'Em Shooting! • Norman Rockwell, 1942, 40½ × 28½
Soldier firing Browning M1917 water cooled machine gun.

Plates 253 Americans All, "...it is the duty of employers and labor organizers to provide for the full participation of all workers without discrimination because of race, creed, color or national origin" Franklin D.Roosevelt speech. War Manpower Commission-Washington, D.C., U.S. Government Printing Office 1942-O -476311 • Anon., 1942, 40 × 28

Plate 254 You Help Build the B-29, U.S. Army Official Poster. I.S.D. No.231, U.S. Government Printing Office 1945-O-438781 • Anon., 1945, 36 × 26

Plate 255 Time to Make Hands Count. Public Works Competition-Bureau of Yards & Docks-Navy Department, Builders for Victory • Anon., ca. 1942, 14 × 22

Plates 256 We Are Working for Something Greater Than $$$. Public Works Competition-Bureau of Yards & Docks-Navy Department, Builders for Victory • Anon., ca. 1942, 14 × 22

Plates 257 Acelere la Construccion. Public Works Competition-Bureau of Yards & Docks-Navy Department, Builders for Victory • Anon., ca. 1942, 14 × 22

Plates 258 Conserve Construction Equipment, by Proper Maintenance & Repair, Bury the Axis. Bureau of Yards & Docks-Navy Public Works Awards-Navy Department • Anon., ca. 1942, 14 × 22

Plate 259 You Knock 'Em Out—We'll knock 'Em Down, More Production. U.S. Government Printing Office: 1942-O-461206, War Production Board A-7 • John Falter USNR, 1942, 28 × 42

Plate 260 Kinda Give It Your Personal Attention, Will You? More Production. U.S. Government Printing Office 443789, War Production Board-A5 • Herbert Roese, ca. 1944, 28 × 40

Plate 261 Miles of Hell to Tokyo! Work Where You're Needed, Consult Your U.S. Employment Service Office. War Manpower Commission, U.S. Government Printing Office 1945 O-646461 • Amos Sewell, 1945, 18 × 26

Plate 262 "God Help Me If This Is a Dud!" His Life is in Your Hands. US Government Printing Office: 1942-O-477498, Ordnance Department, US Army, Keep Em Shooting • John Vickery, 1942, 28 × 40

Plate 263 Keep 'Em Fighting, Production Wins Wars, Stop Accidents, National Safety Council Inc. 7008-C • Anon., ca. 1942, 25 × 37

Plate 264 I'm Proud of You Folks Too! U.S. Government Printing Office 1944 O-577557, Official Navy Poster, Industrial Incentive Division, 6-80M • Jon Whitcomb, 1944, 40 × 28½

Plate 265 Get the Jap and Get it Over!, Work Where You're Needed, See Your U.S.Employment Service, War Manpower Commission. U.S. Government Printing Office 1945 O-648346 • Allen Saalburg, 1945, 20 × 28

Plate 266 Work to Win or You'll Work for Him. Produced for Joint Labor-Management War Production Drive Committee by Rogers-Kellogg-Stillson, Inc, New York • Anon., ca. 1943, 15 × 22

Plate 267 Produce for Your Navy, Victory Begins at Home! "U.S. Navy Dispatch: To fellow Americans ashore: The only way to win this war is to go in there and slug...All of us...all the time. Your job is your battle station: Stay on it...Admiral Ernest J. King, USW, Einson-Freeman Co.Inc • Jon Whitcomb, ca. 1943, 28 × 42

Plate 268 They'll Let Us Know When to Quit! War Manpower Commission, U.S. Government Printing Office: 1942-O-620773 • Lyman Anderson, 1944, 20 × 28

Plate 269 Our Fighters Deserve Our Best. U.S. Government Printing Office: 1942-O-496518 • Anon., 1942, 28 × 40

Plate 270 Bundles for Berlin, More Production! U.S. Government Printing Office: 1942-O-464582, War Production Board, Washington, D.C. A-9 • Melbourne Brindle, 1942, 28 × 40

MORALE AND WHY WE FIGHT

Plate 271 El Nuevo Orden-Del Eje (The New Order-The Axis). Publicado por El Coordinador de Asuntos Interamericano, Washington, E U A • E McKnight Kauffer, ca. 1943, 14½ × 20

Plate 272 Remember Dec. 7th! OWI Poster No. 14, U.S. Government Printing Office: 1942-O-491997 • Allen Saalburg, 1942, 14 × 22, 22 × 28, 28 × 40, & 40 × 56

Plate 273 We French Workers Warn You... Defeat Means Slavery, Starvation, Death. U.S. Government Printing Office: 1942 -O -491777, OWI Poster No. 17 Additional copies may be obtained from the Division of Public Inquiries, Office of War Information, Washington, D.C. • Ben Shahn, 1942, 40 × 28

Plate 274 This is Nazi Brutality, Radio Berlin.-It is officially announced: All men of Lidice-Czechoslovakia-have been shot: The women deported to a concentration camp: the children sent to appropriate centers – The name of the village was immediately abolished. OWI Poster No. 11. issued by the United States Office of War Information. Additional copies may be obtained from the Division of Public Inquiries, Office of War Information, Washington, DC, US Government Printing Office: 1942-O-491104 • Ben Shahn, 1942, 28 × 40

Plate 275 Avenge December 7. OWI Poster No. 15. issued by the United States Office of War Information. Additional copies may be obtained from the Division of Public Inquiries, Office of War Information, Washington, DC, US Government Printing Office: 1942-O-491978 • Bernard Perlin, 1942, 22 × 28 & 28 × 40

Plate 276 Americans Will Always Fight for Liberty, 1778 1943. OWI Poster No. 26. Additional copies may be obtained upon request from the Division of Public Inquiries, Office of War Information, Washington, DC, US Government Printing Office: 1943-O-502684 • Perlin and Martin, 1943, 20 × 28, 28 × 40, and 40 × 56

Plate 277 What Do You Say, America? "We Consider Peace a Catastrophe for Human Civilization" Mussolini. US Government Printing Office: 1942-O-472170, Issued by the Graphics Division, Office of War Information, Washington, DC OWI-P-3 • Anon., 1942, 7 × 10 & 14 × 20

Plate 278 Ten Years Ago: The Nazis Burned These Books ... but Free Americans Can Still Read Them. OWI Poster No. 66. Additional copies may be obtained upon request from the Division of Public Inquiries, Office of War Information, Washington, DC, US Government Printing Office: 1943-O-528869 • Anon., 1943, 20 × 28

Plate 279 What Do You Say, America? "We Shall Soon Have Our Storm Troopers in America" Hitler. U.S. Government Printing Office: 1942-O-472170, Issued by the Graphics Division, Office of War Information, Washington, DC. OWI-P-3 • Anon., 1942, 7 × 10 & 14 × 20
Not shown is the companion poster with Admiral Yamamoto portrait and quote "I am looking forward to dictating peace to the United States in the White House in Washington."

Plate 280 Liberty Lives On, 450th Anniversary of the Discovery of America, 1492-1942. • Howard Chandler Christy, 1942, 26 × 40

SERVICE AND RELIEF ORGANIZATIONS

Plate 281 Help Britain Defend America, Speed Production! Committee to Defend America by Aiding the Allies. • Max Gordon, ca. 1941, 18 × 28

Plate 282 Speed Up America, Committee to Defend America by Aiding the Allies, New York Chapter 8 West 40th St. • James Montgomery Flagg, ca. 1940, 25 × 45

Plate 283 Lest We Regret ... Defend America—Help Britain, Speed Production, Committee to Defend America by Aiding the Allies. • Hawkins, ca. 1940, 18 × 28
The Committee to Defend America by Aiding the Allies (CDAAA) was formed in May 1940, and removed "by aiding the Allies" from its name June 1941.

Plate 284 Britain Must Win, Help Bundles for Britain, National Headquarters 745-5th Ave. New York City. • McClelland Barclay, ca. 1941, 17 × 25

Plate 285 China... Looks to Us! United China Relief. • James Montgomery Flagg, 1945, 14 × 22

Plate 286 China Shall Have Our Help! United China Relief. • Martha Sawyers, ca. 1944, 14 × 22 & 27 × 41
United China Relief was formed in 1941, for the purpose of raising funds to aid the Chinese peoples harmed by war and famine and to inform the US public of the crises and needs in China.

Plate 287 United, the United Nations Fight for Freedom. OWI Poster No. 79, US Government Printing Office: 1942-O-534058 • Leslie Ragan, 1942, 20 × 28 & 28 × 40

Plate 288 The United Nations Fight for Freedom. OWI Poster No. 19, US Government Printing Office: 1942-O-498304 • Broder, 1942, 20 × 28 & 28 × 40

Plate 289 Help British War Victims, the British War Relief Society. Registered with the U.S. State Dept.-No. 208 • Anon., ca. 1942, 14 × 22

Plate 290 British War Relief Society, Help Now! Registered with the U.S. State Dept.-No. 208 • McClelland Barclay USNR, ca. 1942, 17 × 24

Plate 291 The British War Relief Society presents "Thumbs Up", A new film epic the unforgettable story of British Courage, The British War Relief Society, Inc. Registered with the U.S. State Dept.-No. 208, Eloquent Press, N, Morgillo, 460 West 34 St. N.Y. • Anon., ca. 1942, 14 × 22

Plate 292 British War Relief Society, 730 Fifth Avenue New York. Registered with the US State Dept.-No.208 • Frank Kelly, ca. 1942, 15 × 21

Plate 293 Keep Faith with Them, Protect the Families of the Navy's Fighting Men, Navy Relief Society, Navy-Marine Corps-Coast Guard. Litho in U.S.A. • John Falter, USNR, ca. 1942, 12 × 17

Plate 294 Many Campaigns in One, Give Enough for All! Through Your Community Chest • Anon., ca. 1942, 21 × 28

Plate 295 Now Is the Time... Give! United Community and War Fund Campaign • Anon., ca. 1942, 13 × 20

Plate 296 Don't Say "No" to the U.S.O., Give to the USO United Service Organization • Hayden Hayden, ca. 1942, 21 × 11

Plate 297 Join American Red Cross • RC Kauffmann, 1942, 30 × 20

Plate 298 War Relief, Give! American Red Cross • F Sands Brunner, ca. 1941, 13 × 20

Plate 299 Their Fight Is Our Fight, Give Today, United Jewish Appeal for Refugees, Overseas Needs and Palestine • Fodor, ca. 1946, 14 × 22

Plate 300 untitled (Chain Him). Soviet War Poster 1941, reproduced by Russian War Relief Inc. • after Sergei Nikolaevich Kostin, 1941, 28 × 20

PRIVATELY PRINTED

Plate 301 Rumors Cost Us Lives. This poster is published by the House of Seagram as Part of its Contribution to the National Victory Effort, Seagram-Distillers Corp., N.Y.C. • Anon., ca. 1942, 21 × 28

Plate 302 No Room for Rumors. This poster is published by the House of Seagram as Part of its Contribution

to the National Victory Effort, Seagram-Distillers Corp., N.Y.C. • Ess-ar-gee´, ca. 1942, 21 × 28

Plate 303 Starve Him with Silence, War Secrets. This poster is published by the House of Seagram as Part of its Contribution to the National Victory Effort, Seagram-Distillers Corp., N.Y.C. • Ess-ar-gee´, ca. 1942, 21 × 28

Plate 304 Loose Lips Might Sink Ships. This poster is published by the House of Seagram as Part of its Contribution to the National Victory Effort, Seagram-Distillers Corp., N.Y.C. • Ess-ar-gee´, ca. 1942, 21 × 28 *See also Plates 72, 227, 391, and 445.*

Plate 305 Look Who's Listening. This poster is published by the House of Seagram as Part of its Contribution to the National Victory Effort, Seagram-Distillers Corp., N.Y.C. • Essargee´, ca. 1942, 21 × 28

Plate 306 Even in This Friendly Tavern There May Be Enemy Ears, Stop Loose Talk—Rumors. This poster is published by the House of Seagram as Part of its Contribution to the National Victory Effort, Seagram-Distillers Corp., N.Y.C. • Essargee´, ca. 1942, 21 × 28

Plate 307 One Year's Liquor Industry Taxes Could buy 20 Battleships. Remember Prohibition? Don't Let it happen again! Contributed as a Public Service by Calvert Distillers Corp., N.Y.C. Series 1-E • Anon., ca. 1942, 17 × 25

Plate 308 "Come on Pals... Let's Do It Again." Remember Prohibition? Don't let it happen again! Contributed as a Public Service by Calvert Distillers Corp., N.Y.C. Series 1-S • Anon., ca. 1942, 17 × 25

Plate 309 Prohibition "You Can't Hypnotize us Again, Brother!" Remember Prohibition? Don't Let it happen again! Contributed as a Public Service by Calvert Distillers Corp., N.Y.C. Series 2-S • Anon., ca. 1942, 17 × 25

Plate 310 One Year's Liquor Industry Taxes Could Buy 1,236 Bombers. Remember Prohibition? Don't let it happen again! Contributed as a Public Service by Calvert Distillers Corp., N.Y.C. Series 2-E • Anon., ca. 1942, 17 × 25

Plate 311 The Sowers, They Want What We Have! ... and they will take it unless we find some of the Iron that was in the Souls of our Fighting Forefathers! This Painting has been made available in the Public Interest by Abbott Laboratories, North Chicago, Ill. • Thomas Hart Benton, 1942, 23½ × 18 & 40 × 60

Plate 312 Again, "Mastery, not Brotherhood"-"Control, not Share", These are the slogans of Our Enemies! This Painting has been made available in the Public Interest by Abbott Laboratories, North Chicago, Ill. • Thomas Hart Benton, 1942, 23½ × 20 3/4 & 40 × 60

See also Plate 491.

Plate 313 Pride of the Fleet. EBCo Submarine at Periscope Depth Firing Two Torpedoes, Copyright 1943, Electric Boat Company, New York • Wright, 1943, 24 × 19

Plate 314 Revenge in the Pacific. Sinking Jap Ship from Official US Navy Photo Taken Through Periscope, Copyright 1943, Electric Boat Company, New York • Gerald Leake, 1943, 24 × 19

Plate 315 This Is America—For This We Fight, Like Mighty Niagara's Torrents Is the Strong Surge of Our Patriotism. The Majesty of Niagara Falls, The Ullman Co, Brooklyn, N.Y. • Anon., ca. 1943, 20 × 30

Plate 316 This Is America—For This We Fight, External Vigilance Is the Price of Liberty. The Minuteman, Lexington Mass, The Ullman Co, Brooklyn, N.Y. • Anon., ca. 1943, 20 × 30

Plate 317 This Is America—For This We Fight, Links of Steel Unite America. George Washington Bridge, which links New York with New Jersey and the West, The Ullman Co, Brooklyn, N.Y. • Anon., ca. 1943, 20 × 30

Plate 318 This Is America—For This We Fight, Heroes of the Republic—An Inspiration to the Heroes of Today. Mt. Rushmore National Memorial, Honoring Washington, Jefferson, Theodore Roosevelt and Lincoln, The Ullman Co, Brooklyn, N.Y. • Anon., ca. 1943, 20 × 30

Plate 319 What Matters Most Is That They Get Through on Time! Pennsylvania Railroad Serving the Nation. 36,450 in the Armed Forces-66 Have given their lives for their country. Buy U.S. War Bonds and Stamps • Anon., ca. 1942, 25 × 42

Plate 320 You Can Help Save Telephone Service for War Needs, Don't call information for numbers in the directory • Anon., 1942, 25 × 38

Untitled (Axis in Agony), Wickwire Steel

Plate 321 1944
Plate 322 1944
Plate 323 1942
Plate 324 1942
Plate 325 1943
Plate 326 1943
Plate 327 1944
Plate 328 1943
Plate 329 1944

Plate 330 1943
• Boris Artzybasheff, 21 × 17
Multi-year advertising campaign in which the artist discretely used the client's products in each poster.

Philco Radio

Plate 331 Let's Bury the Tramps with Bonds and Stamps. • Walt Ditzen, 1943, 18 × 12

Plate 332 Let's Hit 'em Hard, America. • Sid Hix, 1941 18 × 12

Plate 333 Put Your Money in the Sock. • Walt Ditzen, 1944, 18 × 12

Plate 334 Three Blind Rats! • Rube Goldberg, 1943, 18 × 12

Plate 335 "Look Out Boys...They're Loaded!" • William Sandeson, 1941, 18 × 12

Plate 336 "You Said It, Boys!" • Daniel Bishop, 1942, 18 × 12

Plate 337 Keep 'Em Frying! • Sid Hix, 1942, 18 × 12
Multi-year advertising campaign by Philco Radios. Numerous artists created images that were used in magazine advertisements and separately printed as standalone posters.

Plate 338 It's Great to Be Helping Uncle Sam. The National Safety Council Incorporated Chicago, Printed in U.S.A, 6924 • Ralph Moses, ca. 1944, 9 × 12

Plate 339 "Victory Through Airpower—Peace Through Airpower" Lockheed Aircraft Corporation-Vega Aircraft Corporation. • Anon., ca. 1943, 16 × 17. *This poster was distributed for free by Lockheed and referred to in Lockheed magazine ads as "Illustration from Walt Disney Production 'Victory Through Air Power'".*

Plate 340 A Great Railroad ...In War! The New Haven R.R., For Victory Buy War Bonds and Stamps. • Anon., ca. 1943, 28 × 42

Plate 341 Right of Way for Fighting Might, The New Haven R.R., For Victory Buy War Bonds and Stamps. • Anon., ca. 1943, 28 × 42

Plates 342-345 The Kid, The New Haven R.R. • Anon., ca. 1943, 28 × 42.
Series of posters asking readers, presumably riders of the New Haven Rail Road, to accept any small hardships caused by the war as small compared to those experienced by a fictional "kid" facing the real trials and hardships of war.

Plate 346 Buy More War Bonds and Stamps. Winner R. Hoe & Co., Inc. Award—National War Poster Competition, Held under the auspices of Artists for Victory, Inc—Council for Democracy—Museum of Modern Art, Reproduced through courtesy of R. Hoe & Co., Inc., New York, N.Y., Lithographed in USA on Hoe Super-Offset Press by Grinnell Lithographic Co., New York, N.Y. •

E. B. Greenshaw, 1942, 24 × 36
Winner in the category "Theme B-War Bonds""

Plate 347 This is the Enemy. Winner R. Hoe & Co., Inc. Award—National War Poster Competition, Held under the auspices of Artists for Victory, Inc—Council for Democracy—Museum of Modern Art, Reproduced through courtesy of R. Hoe & Co., Inc., New York, N.Y., Lithographed in U.S.A. on Hoe Super-Offset Press by Grinnell Lithographic Co., New York, N.Y. • Karl Koehler, Victor Ancona, 1942, 24 × 36
Winner in the category "Theme C-Nature of the Enemy"

Plate 348 Accident or Sabotage? Prevent It by Vigilance. Consolidated Edison System Companies. • Anon., ca. 1943, 13½ × 18

Plate 349 Working Together to Defend America, Consolidated Edison System Companies. • Anon., ca. 1943, 13½ × 18

Plate 350 It Can Happen Here. 1942 General Electric Company • Anon., 1942, 38 × 50½

Plate 351 Too Little and Too Late. 1942 General Electric Company • Anon., 1942, 38 × 50½

Plate 352 Prevent This (Swastika branding soldier). 1942 General Electric Company • Anon., 1942, 22 × 30 & 38 × 50½

Plate 353 Step On It! Let's Go, Everybody! Keep 'Em Firing! Oldsmobile Division, General Motors Corporation, Lansing, Michigan, Litho in USA 15 • Anon., 1942, 30 × 40

Plate 354 Thanks, Buddy! Keep 'Em Firing! Oldsmobile Division, General Motors Corporation, Lansing, Michigan, 22 • Anon., 1942, 30 × 40

Plate 355 Our Next Boss? Not if We Keep 'Em Firing! Oldsmobile Division, General Motors Corporation, Lansing, Michigan, 18 • Anon., 1942, 30 × 40

Plate 356 In the Army... Behind the Army, Let's Keep 'em Pulling for Victory. GMC-N Litho in USA • Anon., ca. 1942, 30 × 40

Plate 357 Out in Front on Every Front, Keep 'Em Pulling for Victory. GMC- 47 Litho in USA • Anon., ca. 1942, 30 × 40

Plate 358 The *Saturday Evening Post*, Oct. 4, '41. • Norman Rockwell, 1941, 22 × 28

Plate 359 The *Saturday Evening Post*, Feb. 4, '42. • Norman Rockwell, 1942, 22 × 28
Rockwell created dozens of covers for the SEP during WWII, often featuring military personnel and war themes. These covers were printed as large format posters for display at locations selling the magazine. See also Plate 114.

Plate 360 Loose Talk Can Cost Lives, Keep It Under Your Stetson. • Frank Goodwin, ca. 1942, 30 × 40

Plate 361 The Pack to Take Wherever You Go! Kools, Get War Stamps with B&W Coupons. • Anon., ca. 1942, 20 × 30

MISCELLANEOUS

Plate 362 Cette Fois Jusqú à Berlin, (This time we won't stop until Berlin) US(P)F.10. • Anon., ca. 1944, 40 × 30

Plate 363 Untitled (Allies breaking swastika) U.S.P.F.11. • Frederic Henri Kay Henrion, 1944, 26 × 19
Note that in both Liberated France posters created by the US government, France is given exactly equal placement with the United States, England, and Russia.

Plate 364 Czechoslovaks Carry On • A.T. Peel, 1942, 24 × 32

Plate 365 New Zealand Fights • A.T Peel, 1942, 24 × 32

Plate 366 V Free Czechoslovakia • Anon., ca. 1943, 17½ × 24

Plate 367 Wanted in Prague • Anon., ca. 1943, 17½ × 24

GREAT BRITAIN

Plate 368 "Never Was So Much Owed by So Many to So Few", The Prime Minister. Printed for H.M.

Stationery Office By Lowe & Brydone Printers Ltd., London, N.W. 10. • Anon., ca. 1940, 20 × 30

Plate 369 "Let Us Go Forward Together" Printed for H.M. Stationery Office By J Weiner LTD. London, W.C.I. 51-165 • Anon., ca. 1940, 20 × 30
The phrases "Let Us Go Forward Together" and "Blood, Toil, Tears and Sweat" were both included in Churchill's first speech as Prime Minister to the House of Commons on May 13, 1940.

Plate 370 You Are Wanted Too! Join the ATS. Printed for H.M. Stationery Office by A.C. Ltd, 51-2075 • Anon., ca. 1940, 19 × 30

Plate 371 Join the WRENS, Womens Royal Naval Service, and Free a Man for the Fleet. Printed for H.M. Stationery Office By J Weiner LTD. London, W.C.I. 51-381 • Anon., ca. 1940, 10 × 15 & 20 × 30

Plate 372 Serve in the WAAF with the Men Who Fly. Printed for H.M. Stationery Office By Lowe & Brydone Printers Ltd., London, N.W. 10. 51-1190 • Foss, ca. 1940, 20 × 30

Plate 373 Take the Road to Victory, Join the WAAF. Printed for H.M. Stationery Office by Fosh & Cross LTD., London. 51-1462 • Foss, ca. 1940, 20 × 30

Plate 374 Leaders of the Royal Air Force. Printed by Chromoworks Ltd., London England, ACP 16-8 1941 • Anon., 1941, 30 × 20
Per ardua ad astra ("Through adversity to the stars" or "Through struggle to the stars") is the motto of the Royal Air Force.

Plate 375 The Royal Navy. If your age is from 17½ to 28 and you have at least 2½ years experience in any of the following trades Ground Engineer (Civil Aviation), General Fitter, Millwright, Jig & Tool Fitter, Engine Fitter, Mechanical Transport Fitter, Engine Turner, Blacksmith, Coppersmith, Metal Worker, Why not join the new fleet air arm as air fitter or air rigger? Generous pay and allowances-Really secure employment. Good Prospects of early advancement to air artificer. Ask your post office for the address of the nearest R.N. & R.M recruiting station and write or call for full particulars. Printed for H.M. Stationery Office by Vincent Brooks Day & Sons LTD., London. WCB. 51-3267 • Pat Keely, 1939, 15 × 20

Plate 376 She's in the Ranks Too! Caring for evacuees is a national service. Issued by the Ministry of Health. Printed for H.M. Stationery Office By J Weiner LTD. London, W.C.I. 51-22 • NY (initials) ca. 1940, 20 × 30

Plate 377 A Message from Her Majesty the Queen to the Nurses of Britain. My thoughts go out to the women who, in this third year of War, are serving the cause of humanity in every branch of the Nursing Profession. May you be granted strength and courage to carry on your selfless

labours and may you find your reward in the gratitude of those to whom you minister. Elizabeth R. • Anon., ca. 1943, 10 × 15

Plate 378 Scrap It Before It Scraps You. Issued by the Ministry of Labour and National Service and produced by the Royal Society for the Prevention of Accidents, Terminal House, 52, Grosvenor Gardens, London, S.W.I, Printed by Loxley Bros. Ltd. • Pat Keely, 1942, 20 × 30

Plate 379 Six Health Hints—Keep Fighting Fit. Wash all over, Change all underclothes, Germs of many diseases enter through your mouth, Remove all bedding, Keep the ventilators open, Don't leave litter about. Printed for H.M. Stationery Office by Chromoworks LTD., 51-842 • Anon., ca. 1942, 20 × 30

Plate 380 Splinters Are Poisoned Arrows—Get First Aid. Issued by the Ministry of Labour and National Service and produced by the Royal Society for the Prevention of Accidents, Terminal House, 52, Grosvenor Gardens, London, S.W.I, Printed by Loxley Bros. Ltd. • Pat Keely, 1942, 20 × 30

Plate 381 Blood Donors Are Needed Urgently to Save Lives, Emergency Blood Transfusion Service, Issued by the Ministry of Health. Printed for H.M. Stationery Office by Lowe & Brydone Printers Ltd., London N.W. 10 51-2403 • A Games, ca. 1942, 13 × 19

Plate 382 Post Office Savings Bank, Save for Defence, P.B. 30 • Frank Newbould, ca. 1942, 20 × 30

Plate 383 More Ships—Come on! War Savings are Warships.... WFP172 Issued by the National Savings Committee London, The Scottish Savings Committee Edinburgh, and the Ulster Savings Committee Belfast. Printed for H.M. Stationery Office By J Weiner LTD, London WCI 51-1012 • Anon., ca. 1942, 10 × 15

Plate 384 The Signal Is Save. Issued by the National Savings Committee London, the Scottish Savings Committee Edinburgh, and the Ulster Savings Committee Belfast • Anon., ca. 1942, 10 × 15

Plate 385, Post Office Savings Bank. Save for Victory, P.B. 40 • Frank Newbould, ca. 1942, 20 × 30

Plate 386 Join the Crusade Buy Defence Bonds. W.F.P. 102 Issued by the National Savings Committee London, the Scottish Savings Committee Edinburgh, and the Ulster Savings Committee Belfast. Printed for H.M. Stationery Office By Waterlow & Son LTD., London (51-7721) • Anon., ca. 1942, 10 × 15 & 20 × 30

Plate 387 Keep the Wheels Turning, Repair Work Is Vital to the War Effort. Issued by the Ministry of War Transport, Printed for H.M. Stationery by H. Manly & Son Ltd 51 9656 • Frank Newbould, ca. 1942, 15 × 20

Plate 388 Keep Mum—She's Not So Dumb! Careless Talk Costs Lives. Issued by the Ministry of War Transport, Printed for H.M. Stationery by H. Manly & Son Ltd 51 9656 • AS (initials), ca. 1942, 20 × 30

Plate 389 Keep Mum—She's Not So Dumb! Careless Talk Costs Lives. Printed for H.M. Stationery Office by Graycaine Ltd., Watford and London 51-9976 • Gerald Lacoste (attributed), 1942, 10 × 15 & 20 × 30
See also Plates 476, 477 & 493.

Plate 390 Don't Tell Aunty & Uncle, Or Cousin Jane, and Certainly Not —. • G (Gerald) Lacoste, ca. 1942, 25 × 39½

Plate 391 A Few Careless Words May End in This—Many lives were lost in the last war through careless talk. Be on your guard! Don't discuss movements of ships of troops. Printed for HM Stationery Office by Greycaine LTD, Watford & London T 51-5667 • Norman Wilkinson, ca. 1942, 10 × 15 & 15 × 20
See also Plates 72, 227, 304, and 445.

Careless Talk Costs Lives,

Plate 392 "....Strictly between these four walls!"

Plate 393 Don't forget that walls have ears!

Plate 394 You never know who's listening!

Plate 395 "Of course there's no harm in YOUR knowing!"

Plate 396 "..... but of course it mustn't go any further!!"

Plate 397 "Strictly between you & me....."

Plate 398 Be careful what you say and where you say it!

Plate 399 "......but for heaven's sake don't say I told you!"
• Fougasse (Cyril Kenneth Bird), ca. 1943, 8 × 12½

Plate 400 For Bombs Like These, We Must Have These. Printed for H.M. Stationery Office by Chromoworks Ltd., 51-1342 • Anon., ca. 1942, 10 × 15 & 20 × 30

Plate 401 You Know More than Other People. You are in a position of trust. Don't let the fighting forces down. A few careless words may give something away that will help the enemy and cost us lives. Above all be careful what you say to strangers and in public, Printed for HM Stationery Office by Greycaine LTD, Watford & London T51-6502. • Anon., ca. 1942, 10 × 15 & 20 × 30

Plate 402 We're Waiting to Start as Soon as You Finish. Printed for HM Stationery Office by Greycaine LTD, Watford & London 51-81008 • Anon., ca. 1942, 15 × 20 & 20 × 30

Plate 403 Ports Are Often Bombed When Convoys Are in Because Somebody Talked, Never mention arrivals, sailings, cargocs or destinations to anybody. Printed for HM Stationery Office by Gilbt Whitehead & Co New Eltham S E 9 51-2024 • Anon., ca. 1942, 13½ × 20

Plate 404 You can help to build me a plane, You can learn quickly and you will be working to win. Ask at any employment exchange for advice and full details, a job is waiting for you. Printed for H.M. Stationery Office By J Weiner LTD, London WCI 51-419 • Anon., ca. 1942, 10 × 15 & 20 × 30

Plate 405 You can help to build me a gun, You can learn quickly and you will be working to win. Ask at any employment exchange for advice and full details, a job is waiting for you. Printed for H.M. Stationery Office By J Weiner LTD, London WCI 51-419 • Anon., ca. 1942, 10 × 15 & 20 × 30

Plate 406 You can help to build me a ship, You can learn quickly and you will be working to win, Ask at any employment exchange for advice and full details, a job is waiting for you. Printed for H.M. Stationery Office By J Weiner LTD, London WCI 51-419 • Anon., ca. 1942, 10 × 15 & 20 × 30

Plate 407 If you can't go to the factory help the neighbour who can. Caring for war workers children is a national service. Issued by the Ministry of Health. • Anon., ca. 1942, 19 × 28½

Plate 408 Great Britain will pursue the war against Japan to the very end. Winston Churchill. Printed in England by J. Howitt & Son Ltd., Nottm, 51-1290 • Anon., ca. 1945, 20 × 30

Plate 409 Never in the field of human conflict, have so many owed so much to so few. Winston Churchill, Per Ardua Ad Astra. • FT Chapman, ca. 1940, 17 × 22

Plate 410 Back Them Up! A British "Commando" Raid on a German Held Port in Norway. Printed in England by Fosh & Cross Ltd., London (51-2400) • Anon.

Plate 411 La Gran Breton, Defensora da la Libertad La captura del submarino alemán U 570 por un "Hudson" Lockheed de la Jefatura Costera Británica. The capture of the German submarine U570 by Lockheed (Hudson) of the British Coastal Command • W Krogman

Plate 412 Back Them Up! The bombing in daylight of the power station at Knapsack, Germany, by the Royal Air Force. Printed In England by Chromoworks Ltd., 51-2526 • Leslie James Gardner

Plate 413 Back Them Up! British Field Guns Smash German Tank Attack at Point Blank Range in Libya. Printed for H.M.Stationery Office by James Haworth & Brother LTD, Ltd., London (51-2400) • Harold Pym

Plate 414 Back Them Up! A British Cruiser Ramming an Italian Submarine in the Mediterranean. Printed for H.M.Stationery Office by James Haworth & Brother LTD, Ltd., London (51-2400) • Mark Stone

Plate 415 Back Them Up! A British Tank Attack in the Western Desert. Printed in England by Fosh & Cross Ltd., London (51-2400) • Anon.

Plate 416 Back Them Up! "Hurricanes" of the Royal Air Force, Cooperating with the Russian Air Force. Printed in England by Chromoworks Ltd, London. 51-2326 • Jobson., ca. 1942, 20 × 30
The Back Them Up series included over a dozen posters. Originally printed in English, they were also printed in Spanish, Portugese, French, Arabic, and Persian. These were also printed with a variety of texts promoting the sale of war bonds in several nations.

Plate 417 Together. Printed for H.M. Stationery Office by Lowe & Baydone LTD., London N W 10 51-2010 • Anon., ca. 1942, 20 × 30

Plate 418 Come then let us to the task to the battle and the toil. Each to our part, each to our station, Fill the armies, Rule the Air, Pour out the munitions, Strangle the U-boats, Sweep the mines, Plough the land, Build the ships, Guard the streets, Succour the wounded, Uplift the downcast & Honour the Brave. Let us go forward together in all parts of the Empire, in all parts of this Island. There is not a week, nor a day, nor an hour to be lost. Mr. Winston Churchill, the Prime Minister. Wt. 9097-6,250. Gp.959. 4/41. Printed in England by Fosh & Cross Ltd. • Anon., 1941, 10 × 15

Plate 419 One by One. His Legs Will Be Broken. • E. Kern, ca. 1942, 20 × 30
See also Plate 492.

Plate 420 Carry Your Identity Card Always, You may be asked for it at any time to prove to the Police or Military who you are & where you live. Issued by the Ministry of Health, Printed for H.M. Stationery Office By St Michael's Press LTD, London WCI 51-9542 • Anon., ca. 1942, 10 x15

Plate 421 Buses Give Way to Tanks, Pleasure travelers must give way to war workers! Avoid rush hours. Issued by the Thomas Tilling Group of Companies, England • Anon., ca. 1942, 20 × 30

Plate 422 Travel Between Times, help the workers by avoiding rush-hour travel. Issued by the Thomas Tilling group of companies, England. • Anon., ca. 1942, 20 × 30

Plate 423 The Life-line Is Firm thanks to the Merchant Navy. Printed for HM Stationery Office by St Michael's Press Ltd London 51/1131 • Charles Wood, ca. 1942, 20 × 30

Plate 424 Children are safer in the country... leave them there. Printed in England by Fosh & Cross Ltd., London (51/5527) • Anon., ca. 1942, 10 × 15

Plate 425 Mightier Yet, Britain's Mechanised Army Grows Stronger Every Day. Printed for HM Stationery Office by Greycaine LTD, Watford & London 51-8736 • Harold Pym, ca. 1942, 20 × 30

Plate 426 G R King George's Fund for Sailors, In Aid of the Sailors of all Services, Their Widows, and Orphans, Patron: His Majesty the King. Please send your contributions to HRH The Duke of Connaught, Trinity House London, EC 3, John Waddington Ltd Leeds & London • E Verpilleux, 1947, 20 × 30

Plate 427 untitled (Tanks). W.F.P. 230 Issued by the National Savings Committee London, the Scottish Savings Committee Edinburgh, and the Ulster Savings Committee Belfast, Printed for H.M. Stationery Office By WM. Brown & Co. Ltd. E.C.3. 51-2642 • Anon., ca. 1944, 20 × 30

Plate 428 untitled (Airfield). WFP231 Issued by the National Savings Committee London, the Scottish Savings Committee Edinburgh, and the Ulster Savings Committee Belfast. Printed for H.M. Stationery Office By J Weiner LTD, London WCI 51-2648 • Anon., ca. 1944, 20 × 30

CANADA

Plate 429 The torch; be yours to hold it high! If ye break faith with us who die, though poppies grow in Flanders fields- John McCrae. Issued by the director of Public Information, Ottawa, Under The Authority of Hon. J.T. Thorson, Minister of National War Services, Printed in Canada. UE-2L. • R. Filopowski, ca. 1942, 12 × 18 & 24 × 36

The Canadian National Vimy Memorial, Pas de Calais is dedicated to the memory of Canadian Expeditionary Force members killed during WWI.

Plate 430 Canada's New Army Needs Men Like You. Issued for the Dept. of National Defence by the Director of Public Information, Ottawa • Eric Aldwinckle and Albert E. Cloutier, ca. 1941, 24 × 36

Plate 431 All Aboard! Buy Victory Bonds. • Ken Rowell, ca. 1943, 36 × 24

Plate 432 You Serve by Saving, Buy War Savings Certificates. • Samson, ca. 1942, 19 × 26

Plate 433 Get Out That Tank... Behind the Barn. Farmers Get in Touch with Your Local Salvage Committee. Issued by the Director of Public Information for National Salvage Office, Ottawa, Under Authority of Honourable J.T. Thorson, Minister of National War Services,. Printed in Canada. FS- 2E • Anon., ca. 1942, 12 × 18

Plate 434 It's Got to Fit... to Do Its Bit. Issued by Wartime Information Board, Ottawa, for Department of Munitions and Supply, Printed in Canada. 1E-7 • Anon., ca. 1942, 24 × 36

Plate 435 Roll Out the Rubber, Every Ounce of Scrap Rubber Is Needed for Our Mobile Forces, Get in the Scrap. Issued by the director of Public Information, Under Authority of Hon. J.T. Thorson, Minister of National War Services, Ottawa. For Scrap Rubber Division, Department of Munitions and Supply in Co-Operation with National Salvage Campaign Committee. Printed in Canada. • WBW (initials), ca. 1942, 12 × 18

Plate 436 We're in the Army Now, Your aid is vital. Save metals, rags, paper, bones, rubber, glass. They are used in war supplies. Get in touch with your local committee. Issued by Public Information, for National Salvage Office, Ottawa: Under authority of Hon. J.G. Gardiner, Minster of National War Services. • Anon., ca. 1942, 10 × 15

Plate 437 Save Waste Bones... They Make Glue for Aircraft ... and Are Used for Explosives. • Anon., ca. 1942, 10 × 15

Plate 438 Salvage Bones to Make Glycerine for Explosives, Glue for Aircraft. Issued by the director of Public Information for National Salvage Office, Ottawa, Under Authority of Hon. J.T. Thorson, Minister of National War Services. Printed in Canada. FB-2E • Anon., ca. 1942, 12 × 18

Plate 439 We Want Rags for Vital War Needs! Get in Touch with Your Local Committee. Issued by Public Information, For National Salvage Office, Ottawa; Under Authority of Hon. J.G. Gardiner, Minister of National War Services • Anon., ca. 1942, 10 × 15

Plate 440 Wanted Scrap Metal, to Make Tanks, Guns, Ammunition. Issued by Public Information, For National Salvage Office, Ottawa; Under Authority of Hon. J.G. Gardiner, Minister of National War Services • Anon., ca. 1942, 10 × 15

Plate 441 Dig In and Dig Out the Scrap, Save metal, rags, paper, bones, rubber, glass. They are all vital war needs. Get in touch with your local committee. Issued by Public Information, For National Salvage Office, Ottawa; Under the authority of Hon. James G. Gardiner, Minister of National War Sevices • Anon., ca. 1942, 10 × 15

Plate 442 Housewives! Wage War on Hitler, Save rubber, metal, paper, fats, bones, rags, glass. Issued by the Director of Public Information for National Salvage Office, Ottawa, Under Authority of Honourable J.T. Thorson, Minister of National War Services, Printed in Canada. HS- 2E • Anon., ca. 1942, 12 × 18

Plate 443 Save Waste Paper, It Is Used for Ammunition and Other Vital Needs. Issued by Public Information, For National Salvage Office, Ottawa; Under Authority of Hon. J.T. Thorson, Minister of National War Services • Anon., ca. 1942, 10 × 15

Plate 444 Careless Words May Cause Disaster! Issues by the Director of Public Information Under Authority of Hon. J.T. Thorson, Minister of National War Services, Ottawa, Printed in Canada AG-11ES • Anon., ca. 1942, 9 × 12

Plate 445 Somebody Talked! The Walls Have Ears. Issued by Wartime Information Board, Ottawa Printed in Canada, Design Courtesy of "Walls Have Ears" organization AG-20 • Anon., ca. 1942, 18 × 24 *See also Plates 72, 227, 304, and 391.*

Plate 446 A Workman Gossiped, an Enemy Agent Acted, Don't Talk About Your War Job. Issued by the Director of Public Information, Ottawa. Under the authority of Hon. James G. Gardiner, Minister of National War Services • Anon., ca. 1942, 13½ × 20

Plate 447 He Talked.... This Happened "She sails at midnight..." Careless Talk Costs Lives. Issued by the Director of Public Information, Ottawa. By authority of Hon. James G. Gardiner, Minister of National War Services. • Anon., ca. 1942, 13½ × 20

Plate 448 Shoptalk May Be Sabotalk, The Walls Have Ears. Issued by Wartime Information Board, Ottawa, Printed in Canada, Design, Courtesy Walls Have Ears Organization, AG-18 • Morris, ca. 1944, 18 × 24½

Plate 449 Sealed Lips Will Save Our Ships. Issued by the Director of Public Information, Under Authority, Minister of National War Services, Ottawa. Printed in Canada. AGE 6 • Anon., ca. 1942, 9 × 12

Plate 450 Beware the Walls Have Ears. Issued by Wartime Information Board, Ottawa, Printed in Canada, Design, Courtesy Walls Have Ears Organization, AG-19 • Jac Leonard, ca. 1942, 18 × 24½

Plate 451 untitled (Zipped lips). Printed in Canada-Issued by the director of Public Information, Under Authority of the Hon. J.T. Thorson, Minister of National War Services, Ottawa. Code AG-10E • B (initial), ca. 1942, 16½ × 12½

Plate 452 Anything Less Than Your Best Is Deserting, It's Now or Never on the Production Line. This message is issued by the department of munitions and supply for Canada. • Anon., ca. 1942, 36 × 24

Plate 453 The Lives of These Men Depend on Your Work. Published and distributed under the authority and direction of the Director-General of Aircraft Production, Donated to Canada's War Effort by Canadian Car and Foundry Company Limited • Anon., ca. 1942, 20 × 30

Plate 454 My Needle Hums Along the Track, for Hitler's Ears I'm Pinning Back, Brave Men Shall Not Die Because I Faltered. • Anon., ca. 1942, 18 × 24

Plate 455 If You Don't Need It... Don't Buy It. Issued by the director of Public Information, Under Authority of Hon. J.T. Thorson, Minister of National War Services, Ottawa. Printed in Canada EC1 • M Laren, ca. 1942, 18 × 24½

Plate 456 Thousands Are Waiting to Use What You're Making. This message issued by the Department of Munitions and Supply for Canada • WA Winter, ca. 1942, 18 × 24

Plate 457 Get Your Teeth into the Job. Issued by the Director of Public Information Under Authority of Hon. J.T. Thorson, Minister of National War Services, Ottawa, Printed in Canada UE-6S • Nichol, ca. 1942, 9 × 13½

Plate 458 Nous Luttons Aussi! (We are fighting also!) War time machine shop board, Canadian pulp and paper association. • Anon., ca. 1942, 20 × 30

Plate 459 Pour la Liberté, Tout les Hommes-Tout les Outils (All the men-all the tools) Wartime Machine Shop Board-Canadian Pulp and Paper Association. • Anon., ca. 1942, 20 × 30

Plate 460 It's Our War. 1E-2 Issued by the Director of Public Information, Ottawa, Under Authority of the Minister of National War Services • Aldwinkle, ca. 1942, 21 × 31

Plate 461 Every Canadian Must Fight. Issued by the director of Public Information, Under Authority of Hon. J.T. Thorson, Minister of National War Services, Ottawa. Printed in Canada. UE 35 • Anon., ca. 1942, 12 × 17

Plate 462 Whatever Your Job May Be Fight. Issued by the Director of Public Information, Ottawa, Under Authority of the Minister of National War Services • Anon, ca. 1942, 21 × 31

Plate 463 To Victory. Issued by the director of Public Information, Under Authority of Hon. J.T. Thorson, Minister of National War Services, Ottawa. Printed in Canada. UE-45 • Wilcox, ca. 1942, 9 × 13½

Plate 464 Lick Them over There! Come on Canada. Issued by the director of Public Information, Under Authority of Hon. J.T. Thorson, Minister of National War Services, Ottawa. Printed in Canada UE-5L • Anon., ca. 1942, 12 × 18 & 24 × 36

Plate 465 Let's Go ... Canada! Issued by the Director of Public Information, Under Authority of Hon. J.T. Thorson, Minister of National War Services, Ottawa. Printed in Canada. UE-1S. • Eveleigh, ca. 1942, 12 × 18

Plate 466 Teamwork, Thanks Pal! Published and distributed under the authority and direction of the Director-General of Aircraft Production, Donated to Canada's War Effort by DeHavilland Aircraft of Canada Limited • Anon., ca. 1942, 21 × 31

Plate 467 Lets Go! Step It Up Boys! Prepared and published under the auspices of the Advertising & Sales Club of Toronto and distributed under the authority of the Director-General of Aircraft Production, Donated to Canada's War Effort by MacDonald Bros. Aircraft Limited, Winnipeg, Man • Anon., ca. 1942, 21 × 39

Plate 468 Keep Them Both Flying! Speed Is Vital! Published and distributed under the authority and direction of the Director-General of Aircraft Production, Donated to Canada's War Effort by Northern Electric Company Limited, Montreal • Anon., ca. 1942, 20 × 30

Plate 469 "Daddy Helps Build Them" To Protect Our Freedom. Published and distributed under the authority and direction of the Director-General of Aircraft Production, Donated to Canada's War Effort by British Aeroplane Engines Limited, Montreal • Anon., ca. 1942, 21½ × 33

Plate 470 Roll 'em Out! Published and distributed under the authority and direction of the Director-General of Aircraft Production, Donated to Aluminum Company of Canada, Limited • Anon., ca. 1942, 21 × 31

Plate 471 This means D-E-L-A-Y! This VICTORY. Prepared and published under the auspices of the Advertising & Sales Club of Toronto and distributed under the authority of the Director-General of Aircraft Production.Donated to Canada's War Effort by Fleet Aircraft Limited, Fort Erie, Ont. • Anon., ca. 1942, 39 × 31

Plate 472 Wanted, Magazines for Our Fighting Men, Get in touch with your local committee. Issued by Public Information, for National Salvage Office, Ottawa; under authority of Hon. J. G. Gardiner, Minister of National War Services • Anon., ca. 1942, 10 × 15

Plate 473 Send the Boys Good Books and Magazines. Issued by the Director of Public Information for National Salvage Office, Ottawa, Under Authority of Honourable J.T. Thorson, Minister of National War Services, Printed in Canada. BM- 2E • Clair Stewart, ca. 1942, 12 × 18

AUSTRALIA & NEW ZEALAND

Plate 474 Hold Your Tongue. • Anon., ca. 1942, 8½ × 12½

Plate 475 War on Waste, Save your scrap for the Big Scrap, Inquire from Patriotic or Charitable Organisations or from Local Council or Schools Regarding disposal of collected materials. Issued by the State Controller of Salvage, Mines Dept, Treasury Gardens Melbourne. Melb.: H.E. Daw. Acting Govt. Printer Melb. • Cochrane, ca. 1942, 13½ × 19½

Plate 476 Stick to Your Dancing, Soldier, Tell no troop news in her ear, Japanese gentleman listen near, Stick to your dancing, soldier. SVY/MISC./042 Reproduced by 2/1 Aust. FD. SVY. Coy. R.A.E • Hodge (sp?), 1942, 24 × 26

Plate 477 When You Leave Work Forget It!, Don't tell anyone how much you do, Japanese gentleman like to know too. SVY/MISC./048 Reproduced by 2/1 Aust. FD. SVY. Coy. R.A.E. • Anon., ca. 1942, 22 × 30½
Survey Unit of the Royal Australian Engineers. See also Plates 388, 389, and 493.

Plate 478 Sorry—Australia Got It First! Invest in the 4th Liberty Loan. • Anon., 1943, 19½ × 29½
See also Plate 124.

Plate 479 Our Own Prime Minister Asks You...Buy 4th Liberty Loan. • Anon., 1943, 19½ × 29½

Plate 480 Back the Attack, Invest in the 4th Liberty Loan. • Anon., 1943, 19½ × 29½

Plate 481 Back the Attack, Invest in the 4th Liberty Loan. • Anon., 1943, 29½ × 39½

Plate 482 New Zealand Fights in Pacific Skies, • Anon., 32½ × 24½, ca. 1942,
Issued by the New Zealand Legation, Washington, DC. Printed in USA.

Plate 483 New Zealand Fights for the Future. • Anon., ca. 1941, 28 × 22

LIBERATED FRANCE

Plate 484 Liberation. Liberation La Fayette Nous Voilà. Affiche exécutée sous l'Occupation Allemande. About 1944, Here we are. • R. Dumoulin, 1944, 30 × 45½

Plate 485 Libération. G.P.R.F, Secretariat General a L'Information, Affiche Executee Sous L'Occupation Allemande _ Aout 1944 • Phili, 1944, 30 × 45½

THE AXIS

Plate 486 1934-XII SI (Mussolini). • Xanti Schawinsky, 1934, 26 × 37
This poster was included in the April 1934 issue of the Italian magazine Il Revista Illustrata del Popollo.

Plate 487 Nur Hitler (Only Hitler). Schroff-Druck Augsburge • AG (initials), 1932, 20 × 28½
Campaign poster from the 1932 German presidential election. Adolph Hitler lost the election to incumbent Paul Von Hindenburg, who appointed him Chancellor of Germany in 1933.

Plate 488 Yudan Taiteki (Take Care of Fire -Overconfidence can be a Great Enemy). Donated by Taisho Seima Co. • Anon., ca. 1942, 12 × 28

Plate 489 Rules for Air Defense Apply From April 1. Seminar for "Building rules for air defense" sponsored by Police Department • Anon., ca. 1943, 22 × 32

Plate 490 untitled ($2 Venus de Milo). PAJ I46 • Gino Boccasile ca. 1942, 37 × 50

Plate 491 untitled (American soldier plundering church). • Gino Boccasile ca. 1942, 28 × 40
See also Plate 312.

Plate 492 Confiance... Ses Amputations se poursuivent méthodiquement, (Confidence ... His Amputations continue methodically • SPK (initials), ca. 1942, 31 × 46
See also Plate 419.

Plate 493 Achtūng Spione. Vorsicht bei Gesprächen! (Beware-Spies. Be Careful What You Say!) • Theo Matejko, ca. 1943, 22½ × 33
See also Plates 388, 389, 476, and 477.

THE MARSHALL PLAN
EUROPEAN RECOVERY PROGRAM

Plate 494 Prosperity, the Fruit of Co-Operation, European Recovery Programme • Brian Deer, 1950, 21½ × 29

Plate 495 Wir Bauen ein Neues Europa (We're Building a New Europe) ERP. • Kurt Krapeik, 1950, 21½ × 29

Plate 496 Cooperation Intereuropeanne Pour un Niveau de Vie Plus Eleve (Inter-European Cooperation for Better Living Conditions). • Gaston Van Den Eynde, 1950, 21½ × 29½

Plate 497 Inter-europaische Zusammenarbeit fur bessere Lebensbendingungen (Inter-European Cooperation for Better Living Conditions • Alfred Lutz, 1950, 21½ × 29½

Plate 498 Samen Werk, Samen Sterk (Work Together, Strong Together). • F.J. F. Nettes, 1950, 21½ × 29½

Plate 499 Einiges Europa-Tragtwohlstand, (A United Europe Carries Prosperity). • Walter Hofmann, 1950, 21½ × 29½

Plate 500 La cooperation inter-européenne pour un niveau de vie plus eleve, (Inter-European Cooperation for Better Living Conditions). • Gottfried Honegger-Lavater, 1950, 21½ × 29½

Plate 501 Pour se Soulever et Vivre Mieux (ERP to Raise the Standard of Living). • Alfredo Lalia, 1950, 21½ × 29½

Plate 502 Cooperation Intereuropeenne (Inter-European Cooperation). • Fabien Vienne, 1950, 21½ × 29½

Plate 503 Reconstruire L'Europe (To Rebuild Europe). • Alban Wyss, 1950, 21½ × 29½

Plate 504 Seve Nouvelle Vie Meilleure-Cooperation inter-e uropéenne (Inter-European Cooperation New Sap, Better Life). • Andre Golven, 1950, 21½ × 29½

ENDNOTES

1. "The Price of Freedom: Americans at War," http://amhistory.si.edu/militaryhistory/collection/object.asp?ID=544

2. Museum of Modern Art press release, https://www.moma.org/momaorg/shared/pdfs/docs/press_archives/841/releases/MOMA_1942_0083_1942-11-21_421121-76.pdf

3. Winston Churchill's "Prewar Effort to Increase Military Spending," http://www.historynet.com/winston-churchills-prewar-effort-to-increase-military-spending.htm

4. The George C. Marshall Foundation, http://marshallfoundation.org/marshall/the-marshall-plan/marshall-plan-speech/

5, The National Archives, "Power of Persuasion, Poster Art from World War II," http://www.archives.gov/exhibits/powers_of_persuasion/this_is_nazi_brutality/this_is_nazi_brutality.html

6. "American Treasures of the Library of Congress," http://www.loc.gov/exhibits/treasures/trm015.html

7. Anne Frank Guide, "The use of Terror as a Weapon," http://www.annefrankguide.net/en-us/bronnenbank.asp?oid=18587

8. WWI and Depression, http://www.gilderlehrman.org/history-by-era/essays/great-depression-and-world-war-ii-1929-1945

WI

of V

PLANES OF THE

SHIRTS WI

F4U ★ CORSAIR American fighter

P-40 ★ WARHAWK American fighter

HURRICANE II C ★ British fighter

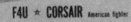
IL-4 ★ STORMOVIK Russian fighter

DB-3F ★ Russian medium bomber

B-25 ★ MITCHELL American mediu